A GUIDE TO PARENTING THE BLENDED FAMILY

THE

FAMILY

PUZZLE

PUTTING THE PIECES TOGETHER

Nancy S. & William D. Palmer
with Kay Marshall Strom

PIÑON PRESS

P.O. Box 35007, Colorado Springs, CO 80935

Library of Congress Catalog Card Number:
96-6006

ISBN 08910-9492

Some of the anecdotal illustrations in this book are true to life and are included with the permission of the persons involved. All other illustrations are composites of real situations, and any resemblance to people living or dead is coincidental.

Palmer, Nancy S.
    The family puzzle : putting the pieces together: a guide to parenting the blended family / Nancy S. & William D. Palmer, with Kay Marshall Strom.
        p.   cm.
    Includes bibliographical references.
    ISBN 0-89109-949-2 (pbk.)
        1. Stepfamilies. 2. Stepparents. 3. Parenting.
I. Palmer, William D., 1952- . II. Strom, Kay Marshall, 1943- . III. Title.
HQ759.92.P33 1996
646.7'8—dc20   96-6006
                                                        CIP

Printed in the United States of America

1 2 3 4 5 6 7 8 9 10 / 99 98 97 96

CONTENTS

ONCE UPON A TIME ...

Divorce really was a rare event, with a social stigma and considerable legal difficulty attached to it. We need not have fantasized, and had no reason to idealize, America's two-parent households — homes where Mom and Dad had met as teenagers, fallen in love, "raised a family," and stayed together for a lifetime. Ozzie and Harriet and "Father Knows Best" reflected an era in which Mom was always home when the kids came home from school, family squabbles were often the result of simple misunderstandings, and adolescent problems were small bumps to cross over on the road to adulthood. The Brady Bunch, which collected kids from an earlier and present marriage in an amusing household mélange, is still today a prime example of the television "situation" comedy — stepparenting played for laughs and smiles. Indeed, blended families have seldom made for commercially successful serious television drama.

About half our nation's children still live in homes composed of both birthparents and full brothers and sisters (the traditional "nuclear family"). The others, to whom this book is directed, do not. According to 1991

Bureau of the Census data, fifteen percent of American children (about ten million kids) lived that year in amazingly heterogeneous, blended families—homes with at least one stepparent, stepsibling, or half-sibling. The numbers have likely increased since then. Add to the mix adopted children, and the increasing number of "extended" families also raising relative or nonrelative children in a formal or informal foster care or guardianship situation, as well as their grandparents living in the home, and you have a mix of family styles of startling diversity. This is something for our nation to understand and celebrate, not criticize.

In the past few years politicians and public policy experts have paid increasing attention to the startling relationship between poverty, childhood social problems, and children growing up in single-parent homes — kids who have no real "Daddy" in their lives. Many child development experts contend that children grow up healthier with the active involvement of both loving fathers (and father-figures) and mothers (and mother-figures) in their homes and lives.

As a child advocate (and, no less importantly, as someone affected by the "divorce revolution" of the 1970's), I know how important it is, preceding and following family breakup, to minimize the adverse impact of parental conflicts on the parties' children so that both fathers and mothers can maintain a positive role in their children's upbringing. Fran Furstenberg, Lenore Weitzman, Andrew Cherlin, Judith Wallerstein, and other American family scholars have eloquently documented what happens to children when parents part—and it is often ugly: psychological and economic stress, children sometimes completely abandoned (financially and physically) by one parent, etc. The Center on Children and the Law at the American Bar Association has for almost two full decades dealt with such brutal legal consequences of divided families as nonpayment of child support and bitter custody/visitation conflict, occasionally arising to parental abduction and child concealment.

Nancy and Bill Palmer know it takes reflection, insight, and hard work to positively address the inevitable confrontations that arise between ex-spouses, between stepparent and stepchild, and between stepmother and biological mother (as well as stepfather/biological father). Stepparents must often adjust to being treated as "second-class" parents, and learn to be diplomats in avoiding competition with their child's biological parents. Such work is unlikely to be portrayed in instructional ways as we visit the "homes" of America's television families. Nancy and Bill know the trauma (and often futility) of relying on the courts to settle parenting conflicts. Nancy's long-term advocacy through the Florida Bar for her state's children, and her expertise as a child-sensitive family mediator, have inevitably led her and her husband to this book. Judges have no magic wand to wave to eliminate the interpersonal problems regularly faced within blended families. It takes, as the following family stories illustrate, sincere effort (what my young son, Roberto, calls "doing your best"), without losing one's sense of humor (which the Palmers surely have not).

Nancy and Bill share with you the real-life examples of couples who have overcome a wide variety of problems faced by blended families. All of us can gain something by seeing how others have coped with similar situations. And, coming away wiser, we can hopefully live happily—or, at least more happily—ever after.

Howard Davidson, J.D.
Director, American Bar Association
Center on Children and the Law

This book is dedicated to our children—
Brent, Nicholas, Michelle, Carley, and
Joanna, who provide the true blessings that
can come from blending families—and to all
children of blended families, in hopes that the
advice we give will help their parents to be as
proud of them as we are of our children.

ACKNOWLEDGMENTS

We gratefully acknowledge the friendship, encouragement, and candid input to this book provided by the following people experienced in dealing with blended families, both personally and professionally: Dr. Deborah Day, Lori Dickerson, Fran Holt, Marsha and Byron Goss, and James and Dottie McMichen. We also acknowledge the input and assistance of school guidance counselor Marilyn Meredith who, in that role, shared her insights and experiences with children of blended families.

Chapter 1

YOU'RE NOT ON YOUR OWN

We've Been There

I t's six o'clock in the evening and all the girls are home. Michelle, who is fixing dinner, calls for Joanna to come and set the table, but Joanna doesn't want to put her pet rabbit back in its cage on the porch and wash her hands. Carley is struggling with her math homework, determined to get it done before dinner. She has a flyer about after-school cheerleading camp tucked in the book beside her. After dinner, she is going to make a plea for adding one more activity to her busy schedule.

"Everyone help me pick up the family room," Nancy calls, as she rushes down the stairs. "We're having a meeting here tonight in an hour and a half. Come on, Carley, sweep up the peanut shells. And Joanna, put that rabbit away, then carry out the newspapers."

A car pulls up outside and Nick gets out. "He's here! He's here!" Carley and Joanna shriek as they run to greet their big brother. Michelle takes the opportunity to turn the radio up several notches.

Bill walks in just in time to answer the ringing telephone. "Hello? Brent? Sure, we can pick you up . . . .

13

Welcome to a typical evening in our blended family.

We know a great deal about the struggles and frustrations, questions and concerns, rewards and blessings of blended families, because that's where we live. But our expertise is more than just personal experience. We are also professionals who deal on a regular basis with the legal and emotional aspects of blended families from many different situations and diverse circumstances.

Our blended family includes a "yours" son, a "mine" son, two "ours" daughters—one by birth and one by adoption—and a teenage girl who is our daughter in every way but legally. We also have a mixed assortment of extended birth families and new families of ex-spouses. Our family tree could be better described as a tangled climbing vine!

PERSONAL EXPERIENCE

Like you, we never started out to have a blended family. When Nancy married the boy next door, her white knight in shining armor, she fully expected to be married to him forever. That's not how it worked out. She was twenty-eight years old when her marriage ended, and she suddenly found herself in the swelling ranks of single parents.

"I had worked hard to put my ex-husband through law school," Nancy says. "Now I figured it was my turn." Her ex-husband told her she would never make it. Nancy worked harder than ever to prove him wrong.

Despite having a young son to raise and a part-time job to hold down, Nancy did prove her ex wrong by not only making it through law school, but immediately landing a good job in a respected law office. Her reward was a lawsuit filed by her ex-husband. "He claimed that since I was now a beginning attorney who would be keeping long hours, and since he was remarried and already set up in a thriving practice, he could provide a better home for Brent than I could. I was fit to be tied!"

The suit never made it to court. Although she was incredibly skeptical about the idea, Nancy agreed to participate in mediation with her ex-husband. The mediator, a mental health expert, stressed the importance of having both parents involved in two-year-old Brent's life. "This was ten years before the concept of shared parenting was introduced in Florida, so I was under no legal obligation to cooperate," Nancy says. "But then, we weren't coming from a legal perspective. We were coming from the perspective of two parents who truly cared about our child."

From Nancy's years of training and work with handicapped children, it made perfect sense to her to have both herself and her ex-husband involved in little Brent's life. "I had taught many kids whose dads were not a part of their lives. I had seen the results of those kinds of families firsthand, and I knew they were not good."

Nancy's agreement to share parenting with Brent's father was enough to ease her ex-husband's fears that he was going to be squeezed out of his son's life. Looking back, Nancy says, "It was the best decision I ever made."

Although Nancy longed to live in a family with a husband who would share her life and help raise her son, she didn't go out actively looking for someone. Life with another husband and whatever children he might bring to the family seemed far too complicated.

And then it happened. We met, fell in love, and married. We started our life together with two six-year-old sons, Brent (Nancy's son) and Nicholas (Bill's son). We knew right away that we wanted a child together, and fourteen months later, our daughter Carley was born.

In our eyes, our family was perfect. Never mind that the odds were stacked against the survival of our blended family. Certainly no one gave us any specific input or guidance on blending our families successfully, and no one suggested any follow-up or counseling to help us over the rough spots. We were on our own.

PROFESSIONAL EXPERTISE

We began our life together as two professionals involved in extremely high pressure careers. In our second year of marriage, we and our sons were attending a retreat for family lawyers. Seven-year-old Nick ran up to us with a new friend in tow and announced: "This is Nancy, my stepmom. She's a lawyer for families and children. And this is my dad. He's just a plain law lawyer."

It wasn't long before we were both involved in family law, and we have remained involved ever since. Bill's focus moved toward the selection and training of judges who could meet the needs of children and families. Nancy's turned to training judges and to mediation. In her role as a mediator, she has dealt with over 500 families going through divorce, not including the people she represented in ten years of family practice.

Of course, your situation isn't going to be just like ours. We realize you may be facing challenges and concerns we didn't have to deal with. Every blended family is unique, yet there are elements common to all of us. That's where our professional experience comes in. We can guide you through many of the inherent difficulties of blended families and help you avoid the pitfalls that trip up so many unsuspecting couples. We can offer you the professional and practical assistance we lacked in our early years as a blended family.

However your family came about—through divorce and remarriage, the death of a spouse and remarriage, a baby born out of wedlock, adoption—we want you to know that it can blend successfully. We know. We have seen it happen again and again and again. It happened to us.

Our nine-year-old adopted daughter, Joanna, has gone through particularly difficult times. Although she has a birth mother in Romania, we are the only nurturing parents she has ever known. Not long ago we received this letter from her:

Dear Nancy,

I love you very much. You have the best loving, caring heart because you and Bill are the best loving people. And Bill and Nancy, you people are just the best friends and parents.

Love, Joanna

You say you haven't been a successful family so far? You say the challenges of your situation are too daunting? You think you've made some pretty bad mistakes? We say, "Join the crowd." Take responsibility for those mistakes and forgive yourself. Then pick yourself up and prepare to move forward in a more positive direction.

Now is the time to plant the seeds of a happier, healthier family. As you nurture those seeds toward maturity, get ready to receive the unique blessings that only blended families know.

Chapter 2

DEFYING GRIM STATISTICS

*Practical Advice for Blending
Your Family Successfully*

"My nephew attends a small, private junior high
school," Lori told us. "His class took a poll of
how many students lived in blended families
or whose parents were divorced. Out of the sixty kids in
the school, only three lived with their biological mother
and father. My nephew told his parents, 'You don't know
how out of place I am!'"

Certainly this is no scientific statistic, and we're not
suggesting it is reflective of the country as a whole. But it
does say something about the times and society in which
we live.

You may be saying, "Well, there's one good thing
about blended families. Success has to be easier the second time around. I mean, I learned so much the first time.
A second marriage *has* to be easier."

Sorry. Statistics tell us that second marriages fail at an
even greater rate than first marriages. And there's more
bad news: Second marriages that require the blending of
"yours, mine, and ours" children fail at an even *greater*
rate. Judith Wallerstein, in her landmark study on the

effects of divorce on children, noted that half the children in her study saw at least one parent get a second divorce within a decade of the first divorce. Unfortunately, blending and reblending is becoming the American way.

When people remarry, they think they are starting all over again. But too often, they drag the same difficulties and dysfunctions into the next family. They make the same mistakes all over again.

"Great!" you say. "So what chance does my blended family have?"

Actually, you have an excellent chance. The very fact that you are reading this book shows your determination to solidify and strengthen your family. As we look together at some of the difficulties encountered by many blended families, we will explore ways to prepare for them and discuss techniques for dealing with them as they arise.

DISPLACED PEOPLE

"I'll never forget the day I took out my journal and made this frustrated entry," Nancy recalls:

What a day! Within an hour, both Brent and Nick accused Bill of favoring the other. (Bill says he must be doing something right or they wouldn't both come to this conclusion!) We can't win. If we give one a dollar more than the other, or if we buy one a different outfit, they focus on that difference.

Yes, kids certainly do focus on the differences—and so do moms and dads. Actually, it's not difficult to see why. One of the most frustrating dynamics of a blended family is that everyone moves out of his or her accustomed position. Oldest kids may no longer be oldest. Only kids are no longer onlies. Men and women used to having the final say and doing things their own way suddenly have to consider the desires and opinions and biases of someone else.

Divorce or death brought about changes of its own, and the family had to adapt to those changes. Now, with a remarriage, and the resulting blended family, everyone is displaced once again.

"That's exactly what happened to me," Nancy recalls. "My dad died when I was seven years old. As the oldest child, I was head of the household while my mother was at work. She depended on me. I was important. Then when I was nine, my mother remarried. Suddenly I was just a child again. My special place of responsibility had been usurped by a stepfather, and I didn't like it one bit. No way was I going to call this intruder 'Dad.' He was 'Larry,' and I kept him at arm's length. If Larry was hurt by my actions, he never let it show. He was always so loving and giving that in spite of myself, my heart changed. And the day came when I lovingly and willingly called him 'Dad.'"

It is especially difficult for an adolescent or teenager to accept a new father or mother into the family.

"'He's not my dad!' was my daughter's war cry from day one," Marianne said. "She would yell, 'I have a dad, and it's *not him!*' Those explosions hurt us all, but they hurt Peter the most because he was trying so hard to be a good stepdad."

The best way we can help our kids adjust to the role changes is to model adjustment for them. What they see us do will mean infinitely more than what they hear us say.

In our house, there are few lines drawn between mother and father roles. We both go out to work, and we both stay with the kids when the other is out for a meeting or an appointment or away at a conference. We both do what needs to be done around the house, whether it's cooking or laundry or cleaning the bathrooms. It's not the way we were raised, nor is it the way things were in our first marriages. But as single parents, the old "your job and my job" stereotypes were blown away.

"I never worked outside the home before my divorce," one woman in her late forties told us. "At first I hated it. But earning respect in the marketplace has done so much for my self-esteem. And I've grown a great deal as a person. Now in our blended family, my paycheck is really needed. Sure, I'll keep working."

"In my first family, we followed the roles our parents had set," a man in his late thirties told us. "My wife was the nurturer, the housekeeper, the cook. I was the wage earner. My divorce changed all that. For eight years I was a single parent. Now in my second marriage, I am the chief cook because I get home at 4:30 and my wife doesn't get home until 6:00. We do the dishes together."

An older man who married a widow with three teenagers said, "Guess what? You *can* teach an old dog new tricks! I never dreamed I'd be doing all the things I'm doing in this family, but I am, and it works for us."

No one likes to be displaced, neither children nor adults. Getting shoved out of our familiar roles can feel most uncomfortable and upsetting. But by definition, a blended family requires adjustments. Perhaps a good place to start adjusting is by acknowledging that everyone in the family has rights and responsibilities.

Each person in your family has the right to:

✤ love and nurture parents, stepparents, children, stepchildren, grandparents, in-laws, and other family members without harassment. Each one also has the right to be loved by those people.
✤ expect courtesy and respect from other members of the family.
✤ participate in and attend special activities in which other family members are involved, even if those members are not living with them and have no legal rights.

❖ follow his or her beliefs and hold to his or her values and standards without interference from others.

❖ have his or her private life.

In a blended family, everyone has to be flexible, for everyone is struggling to preserve the love and security so vital to his or her well-being. Kids unreasonably accuse their parents of being unfair. That's just the way it is. Determine that in your family, you will be patient with each other. As an adult and a parent, you must be ready to lead the way.

PARENTING ADJUSTMENTS

All families seem to struggle with schedules. But in blended families, where one or both parents share parenting with ex-spouses, balancing the calendar can be a real challenge. You say you and your ex have already worked out special times such as holidays, vacations, and birthdays? Great. That's a good start. But what about stepmother's birthday? Or half-brother's birthday party? Typically Mom gets Mother's Day and Dad gets Father's Day, but what if there is a really important stepparent in your child's life? And speaking of birthdays, which family gets to have a party on the child's special day? Take it from us, a schedule set up ahead of time can save a lot of anger, resentment, hurt feelings, and poor parenting.

For instance, when you set up your schedule, you might agree that one parent will celebrate the weekend before the child's birthday and the other the weekend after. (Your child will love this two-party plan! But be aware that two birthday parties may well be too much, and you can't invite those special friends twice.) You could avoid the party problems by alternating who gives the party—one year with one family, the next year with the other family.

Stereotypical "Disney World Dads" are fast disappearing. Fathers are no longer satisfied to be relegated to nothing but fun-time parents. They want to have real involvement in their children's lives. They want to participate in the wash-your-hands-before-you-eat, finish-your-spinach-or-no-dessert, did-you-get-your-homework-done? type of parenting.

Over the past several years, much of the country has moved in the direction of shared parenting. The assumption now is that all parents want to participate in the day-to-day rearing of their children. To reflect this change, we need to use more appropriate wording. Instead of talking about "custody," we should talk about "residential parent." Instead of talking about "visitation," we should talk about "contact time" or "time sharing."

Our state, Florida, has a list of twelve factors that the court takes into consideration when deciding disputes about who the primary residential parent will be. One factor at the top of the list is: "Which parent is most likely to allow the other parent to participate fully in shared parenting?" The parent committed to shared parenting is the one most likely to become the primary residential parent.

Florida is not alone. In California, for instance, it is presumed that frequent and continual contact with both parents is best for the child. "The designation of physical custody is meaningless and ambiguous in California," an attorney from Los Angeles told us. "The actual custodial schedule means much more than the physical custody designation."

In Texas, too, the "custody" title means little. It is the actual schedule that matters. Texan parents are coming up with creative arrangements, such as the kids staying with dad during the day and with mom at night. Or the children staying with one parent during the work week and with the other on weekends. Or the children moving between houses every other week. An Austin attorney said that in Texas, "mediation is paving the way to a more flexible and varied approach to parental child-care by popularizing creative arrangements that courts are slower to try."

Two types of custody are authorized in Georgia law—physical and legal. Physical custody has to do with where the child lives, while legal custody determines who has the legal ability to make major decisions in the child's life. Any combination of these two types of custody can be agreed upon by the parents or can be awarded by the court. For example, there can be a sole physical and legal custody, where the child lives with one parent and that parent also makes all the important decisions. Or there can be sole physical custody and joint legal custody, where the child lives with one parent but both parents share in the major child-rearing decisions. Or there can be joint legal and physical custody, where both parents spend the same amount time with the child and also share legal custody. "Judges are willing to accept most any kind of custody arrangement the parents agree upon, as long as it is in the best interest of the child," an attorney from Smyrna, Georgia, reports.

Lori knows the value of shared parenting from personal experience. She married a man who had taken an active part in the rearing of his daughters from the time they were infants. "Much of my success in our blended family is based on the bonding my husband did with those children at a very young age," she insists. "The girls were so well bonded with their father that it made it much easier for me to walk in and assume a parenting role with them. They were comfortable with us because they had spent so much time with both parents."

Whatever the legalities in your state, psychologically sound shared parenting means more than who your child lives with when. It means that you and your ex-spouse make joint decisions about all things that affect your child—gymnastics classes, scouts, music lessons, sports involvement, after-school activities, medical and dental care, orthodontia, and all the rest. It means sharing the cost of the countless aspects of raising a child, sharing the help and encouragement a child needs, sharing the transportation from here to there to everywhere. It means attending games and recitals and school conferences. It also means mom and dad consulting on a regular basis. For if you make decisions concerning your child together, you are far more likely to cooperate in carrying them out.

For mothers who are still stuck in the What's-in-it-for-me? mode, consider this: According to the U.S. Census Bureau, the 8 percent of divorced fathers involved in shared parenting pay 90.2 percent of the child support payments assigned them. The 55 percent who have regular access to their children pay 79.1 percent of their support. The 37 percent with neither shared parenting nor access pay only 44 percent of their support.

On every level, and for everyone involved, shared parenting makes good sense.

PARENTING MEETINGS

"Maybe, but it's not going to happen for us," you may be saying. "My ex and I have really big differences between us. How are we going to work them out?"

You probably won't. If you couldn't change one another's personalities and behaviors while you were married, it's pretty unrealistic to think you will be able to do it after your divorce. But what does that have to do with anything? Consulting with your ex only has to do with matters that affect your children. The purpose is to share information about their lives, their activities, where they need help, concerns about their development. You might tell your ex, "Johnny seems to be really hyper this past month. Have you noticed the same thing?" or "Susie wants to take ice skating lessons. It will cost a fair amount, and one of us will have to take her back and forth to the ice rink. But it seems really important to her. What do you think?" With few exceptions, parenting meetings are best kept between the two parents of the child. Stepparents are not included. "Getting together with the other parent's new spouse might sometimes work if the point is simply to state concerns and clear the air," Bill says. "But it works much better if the new spouse gives input to the parent and then lets the parents work it out. If you've got a problem with your spouse's ex-spouse, hash it out with your spouse and let him or her hash it out with the ex." If a situation comes up where you all need to get together, it's a good idea to do it in the presence of a neutral third party, such as a counselor or mediator.

"I have been both the primary residential parent and the secondary residential parent for my son," Nancy says. "I know I didn't always do everything right. But I can say that when I was the primary residential parent, I tried very hard to include my ex in the decision making. When we decided Brent would live primarily with his dad, the tables suddenly turned, and I got a clear picture of just how important joint decision making is. For instance, I learned after the fact that Brent was going to a different dentist. Changing dentists wasn't really a big problem, and there were good reasons for the change. The problem was, I hadn't been consulted about it. If I had, I could have pointed out that it didn't make good financial sense, because Bill's insurance covered the work done by Brent's regular dentist 100 percent. The new dentist wasn't covered in the same way."

One of the most difficult things for a parent to share with an ex-spouse is a separation or divorce in a subsequent marriage. "It's a private matter that has nothing to do with my ex," the parent may insist. Certainly no one wants to share another failure. However, without this information, the other parent won't know how to comfort the child or answer his questions.

UNITED YOU STAND

You share parenting with your ex, but you and your spouse parent together. You are a partnership.

Do you want to know the secret to successful partnership parenting? Here it is: *Stick together.* Always. At all times and in all matters. When you're confident and when you're shaky. When you're positive and when you're unsure. If you determine that from this day on the two of you will always present a united front, no one will be able to pry you apart or play one of you against the other.

"On day one, my husband made it clear to everyone, both directly and indirectly, that I would be an important part of every decision in our blended family," Lori said. "He informed the children he had no intention of making a decision without me. And he never did. Whether it was a simple request or an important matter, his answer was always the same: 'Did you talk to Lori about it? What did she say? Lori and I will discuss it, then we'll give your our answer.' The kids were never given the chance to trap us between them."

What a wise way to blend a family. Make your overall philosophy that of a unified front. Make it clear that the two of you are in this marriage for the long haul. Before long the children will get the message: "This new family member is not going anywhere. He (she) means so much to Dad (Mom) that I will never be able to break them apart." The sooner the children reconcile themselves to your unity, the more quickly you can get on with the process of successful blending.

A united front is especially important when it comes to discipline.

"Mom doesn't make us do that at her house!" Have you heard some version of that one? I think we all have. A good response is: "That's her decision. But your stepmother and I want it done this way in this house."

"But what if I don't agree with a decision my spouse made when I wasn't home?" you may ask.

Support it anyway. You may feel like saying, "You grounded him for *how long?* Well, we'll just see about that!" But bite your tongue. So long as you are in front of the child, support your spouse. Once you get behind closed doors, you can say, "I can't believe you did that!" Then you can disagree and argue and hopefully come up with a compromise. But don't do it in front of the kids.

In many families, one parent will tell the other, "You can do that with *your* kids if you want to, but you're not going to do it with *my* kids!" What a killer message that sends. And it opens up a hole where the kids can get in and begin to dismantle your family.

We realize it's hard to discipline another person's child. Stepparents are in a difficult place. On the one hand, they love their spouse's child, they are impacted by the child's behavior, and they want the child to grow up healthy, physically and emotionally. On the other hand, they fear that if they discipline in a way that makes one of the birth parents uncomfortable, it will put a strain on their relationship with their spouse. What to do? If you find yourself in this position, talk it over with your spouse. Decide together on your family rules and set down acceptable punishments for when those rules are broken. Then determine that should a problem arise, it will be dealt with immediately.

"I never tried to be a father to my adolescent step-daughters," James said. "I only tried to be their friend. One girl appreciated it and the other rejected me. She resented the fact that I was in the house at all. But we let her know that, like it or not, I *was* there, and I was going to be there for a long, long time."

James was wise. He made himself available to both his stepdaughters. If either one had a problem or needed help with something, she could come to him and he would help her. But he was very careful not to push himself onto the girls. They both accepted his help, but only one accepted him.

HOLD YOUR GROUND

"Times have changed, Mom. Things aren't like they were when you were young, Dad. Come on, get with the times!"

You know what you expect from your kids. You talk to them and try to make them understand. Yet they laugh and tell you how hopelessly old-fashioned you are.

It's hard to hold your ground with young people. They pay more attention to what their friends say than to what you say. They laugh at your warnings because they believe they are invincible. Their arguments are convincing because they believe them so completely.

Don't cave in. After all, you are the one with experience. Once you and your spouse have determined the rules and standards of your home, it's up to you to hold fast to them. You want the kids to like you, to see you as a friend, as someone who understands them. If it happens, great. But please know that your young people need a caring, consistent parent more than they need an adult buddy.

A big part of discipline is allowing your kids to experience the consequences of their actions. If they have to suffer through the sunburn ("No sunscreen, Dad. I want to get a quick tan") or freeze through an evening concert ("I just *can't* wear a sweater, Mom. It wouldn't go with my outfit!"), they may be more open to listening to your suggestions next time.

Your goal is not to *drive* your kids, it is to *lead* them. If you try to drive them, you will probably succeed only in driving them away. If you lead them, you will be modeling appropriate behavior they can follow throughout their lives.

Because James worked from home and his wife worked away, he was the one usually in charge of his stepdaughters. "I never tried to force them to do anything," he told us. "I never used threats or ultimatums. What I did was act more like a negotiator. I'd say, 'If you want to go to your friend's house, you've got to get your homework done first .' Then it was up to her. If she really wanted to go, she would do her homework. If she didn't do it, I figured she didn't want to go that badly, and she stayed home. Either way it was her decision."

That is a wise approach. If you hand down ultimatums, you end up jamming yourself into a corner, especially when you are the newcomer to the family. The child might well turn on you and demand, "Who are you to tell me what to do? I hate you!" Then what are you going to do? It is so much more effective to give the child choices and then let him be responsible for the decisions he makes.

AND IF THEY REFUSE?
Punishment is hard for all families, but for blended families it is a special challenge. Perhaps the following Do's and Don'ts will help you find your way.

DO
1. vary your disciplinary techniques. A time-out may be appropriate sometimes, but at other times no television may work better.
2. focus attention on the specific misbehavior that upsets you without bringing up earlier misdeeds.
3. recognize and reinforce correct behavior. ("Thank you for setting the table without being asked. I really appreciate it.")
4. be consistent and firm in carrying out any punishments. Empty threats are far worse than ignoring the behavior in the first place.
5. keep the punishment specific. ("No telephone calls or going out for one week" is better than, "You are grounded!")
6. let your children experience the natural consequences of their misbehavior without you

interfering. ("You didn't get your homework done? No, I will not write a note to your teacher. It's your problem, and you will have to deal with it.")

7. make punishments last for only a limited period of time. ("You cannot go out with your friends for the weekend" is better than "You cannot go out with your friends again until I say you can.")

8. practice both patience and understanding when you are confronted by misbehavior. Remember that the kids are just kids, and there are some pretty tough things going on in their lives.

9. adjust your discipline and punishment strategies to reflect the ages and maturity levels of your children. Being sent to bed at 8:00 may be appropriate for an eight-year-old, but not for a teenager.

10. put the punishment into effect as soon as possible after the inappropriate behavior. Immediate consequences emphasize the relationship of cause and effect that you want your children to understand.

DON'T

1. get involved in a no-win power struggle with your children. ("You will sit in this chair until you eat your dinner!" is a no-win power struggle. It's much better to say, "If you won't eat your dinner, you may be excused from the table. But there will be no snacks this evening.")

2. react to everything your children do that displeases you. Some things are best ignored, so choose your battles.

3. overuse "I" messages ("When I was your age, I had to . . ."). Your children will quickly get

tired of hearing about you and your hardships, or about you and your unfailing wisdom.
4. fail to recognize that each child is different. Each has different strengths and weaknesses, and reacts to things in different ways. Personalities are neither good nor bad. Each has positive applications and negative.

It's tough to make adjustments. When under stress you are sure to say and do things you later regret. We certainly did. Start immediately to establish a pattern of saying "I'm sorry" and "I love you." Be quick to say, "You are forgiven"—and mean it. When someone is forgiven, that's the end of the matter; you don't keep bringing it up. Sure, that person may have to live with the consequences of the action, but that, too, can be a maturing influence.

Nancy likes to tell couples in mediation, "What we're doing here today is redefining the family." That's what blended families are all about—putting the family puzzle together in a different way. The family units you used to have are no more. Now you are a new unit. What you do as a couple will influence your children for the rest of their lives. If you are loving and kind, your kids will notice. Someday their spouses and their children will notice, too. They will see it in the relationships you have built.

PREPARE TO SUCCEED

What does it take to blend a family? It takes two people who are committed first to each other, and second to making the family work. Are you and your spouse truly committed to one another? Are you determined to stick with this new family through thick and thin? Where the family is concerned, are you *committed to success?*

"Our blended family included six teenagers," Fran said. "We came to the point where it was literally us against the kids. But my husband and I were committed to our family. We determined we *would not* let our children drive us apart. One day we overheard one of the kids complaining about us to another: 'You try to ask one of them something and you're talking to both of them! You can't talk to them separately and get them to answer a simple question!' My husband and I looked at each other and sighed with relief. We knew then that we had succeeded."

"Hey," you may say, "divisions and resentments and in-fighting happen in intact families, too. So what makes blended families different?"

You're right, of course. But in an intact family, mom and dad are in the family on an equal basis, and the children aren't trying to rip them apart. New people entering the family are going to be challenged. Kids are especially likely to try to get an "intruding" new spouse out. They figure, "No contest. Mom (or Dad) will always side with me! She (he) has always been there for me, so why would it change now?" Since the adjustment is more difficult for the new person coming into the family, it's up to the established parent to firmly communicate to the children: "I love you just as much as ever, but I am not going to take your side in this. Please don't put me in that position. If you do, I will side with my spouse."

START OUT PREPARED TO SUCCEED.

The best way you can tip the statistics scales in your favor is to be prepared for the trouble spots. Dottie and James said, "The entire time we dated, the girls were included in everything we did. If they wanted to come along, they were welcome. If not, that was their choice. We wanted them to know from the very beginning that they were an important part of the family."

Not everyone will want to be that inclusive. But with any family change, it is important to prepare everyone who will be affected by it. When we were getting ready to adopt Joanna, we were careful to prepare our children for the addition, especially Carley, since she would be the one most affected. During the wait for our new daughter to be allowed out of Romania, Nancy, and Nancy's mother and sister, were at a Mother's Day banquet with five-year-old Carley. While the adults were talking, Carley slipped away from the table and went up to the minister's wife with an urgent request. "Please," she asked, "would you pray for my sister in Romania?"

Preparation doesn't just happen. It takes deliberate planning.

PREPARATION STEPS

As you prepare to make changes in your family—a new marriage, stepchildren coming to live with the family, a new baby, an adoption—it will help to keep these suggestions in mind:

Talk to your children, but don't give them the responsibility for making the final decision. These are adult decisions. Tell the children what is going to happen ("Peter and I have fallen in love, and we want to start a new family. Of course, you will be a very important part of that new family.")

Include the children from both sides in your wedding. It was important to us to have both Nick and Brent involved in our ceremony. No matter how expensive or how simple your wedding, the children should be a part of it. They are also getting married. The blended family will be their new family, too.

If at all possible, meet your ex-spouse's new partner. Getting to know your child's new stepparent will relieve you of a lot of fears. You probably wouldn't be willing to leave your child with a baby-sitter you don't know, so why would you be willing to have your most precious treasure co-parented by someone you have never even met? Some people say, "That isn't necessary, because my child won't be going over there unless my ex is home." Not only is that an illegal restriction, it is totally unrealistic. And even if you could enforce it, what kind of message would that send to your kids? You don't have to become great friends with that other person. You don't even have to like him or her. Just establish a precedent of openness and a willingness to communicate. The unknown breeds fear, and fear feeds terrible behaviors.

Try to eliminate as many unknowns as possible. Be open and forthcoming with everyone. Allow your children to ask questions, then answer those questions as fully and as honestly as you can. Make it a rock-bottom rule that you will disclose to your current spouse all your parenting obligations, both of money and of time.

COMMUNICATION

It's true in intact families, and it's even more true in the increased intricacies of blended families: relationships are built on communication.

Effective communication seldom comes naturally. It usually takes determination and effort. Remember playing the telephone game when you were little? Everyone sat in a circle, and one person started a message by whispering it to the next person. That person whispered it to the next, that one to the next, and so on around the circle. By the time the message got all the way around, it was no longer recognizable, and everyone fell over laughing at the distorted communication. That's what happens within the various branches of most blended families—except that it is no laughing matter. Perhaps an overheard judgment is passed along ("He is so selfish!"), or maybe a snide remark ("That's just another of your mother's harebrained schemes").

Family communication starts with communication between you and your spouse. The way you communicate with each other sets up a pattern for the way your children will communicate with you. You are teaching them by example how to handle dialogue and conflict.

When you talk together, make every effort to be non-judgmental. Send "I" messages as much as possible ("I'm uncomfortable with the way you handled Jessica's discipline. I would have made sure the punishment was enforced," rather than, "When Jessica left without cleaning her room, you should have made her come back and do it. What kind of parent are you?"). Judgmental you-should-have messages will immediately put the other person on the defensive.

One more caution: Covenant together that if at all possible, you and your spouse will resolve any disputes before you go to sleep. Harbored anger becomes progressively more unreasonable and difficult to deal with, and it grows and gains strength as time goes on.

Communication extends to your ex's house. If you are having a problem with your child, it's likely that your ex is also having that problem. You may be saying, "But if I talk to my ex about a problem at our house, she will say I'm doing something wrong." Perhaps, but perhaps not. There is a good possibility she will say, "The same thing is happening here. How shall we handle it?" If she is accusatory, simply respond, "I'm not a perfect parent, but I'm doing the best I can. Can we work together to help our child with this?"

The ideal family situation is one where every family member feels free to say whatever needs to be said, openly and without fear of reprimand, retaliation, or retribution. Whether in a family meeting or in private, your children should feel comfortable expressing their feelings to you.

"I so appreciated James's reaction to my children's orneriness," Dottie told us. "He was mature while understanding that the girls were still immature. When they yelled, 'You're not my dad!', it hurt him deeply, yet he didn't react. I would cry in our bedroom at night, and he would comfort me, saying, 'They're just kids. They'll get over it.' And he was right, they did."

MORE TECHNIQUES FOR BLENDED FAMILIES

Are you anxious for your family to get closer? Here are some techniques that helped us blend our family. We now recommend them to our clients:

Have regular dates together. We can hardly talk about important issues in our home, not even in our own bedroom. With five kids, someone is always knocking on the door, and the telephone is forever ringing. If we want uninterrupted time, we have to get away. So every few weeks we try to go out to dinner or to breakfast to talk about the family, about ways to handle discipline, about counseling needs and financial considerations, sometimes even about what to buy someone for a birthday gift. We've dealt with everything from a child smoking to where we should go for family vacations during these times alone together.

If money is a concern, come up with creative dates. For one date during tight budgetary times, Bill packed a picnic supper and took Nancy to a park, then to a drive-in movie complete with popcorn he had popped and brought along. It cost $3. Some couples walk together in the evening. While they are getting exercise and reducing stress, they talk about the family.

Go one step further and get away for a weekend once a quarter. It is a wonderfully effective way to rejuvenate and gain strength. Too expensive, you say? Not necessarily. If you can't afford baby-sitting, work out a deal with another couple to trade off. And you don't have to go to an expensive place. Some hotels run weekend specials because most of their business comes in during the week. We have friends who get away by packing up their tent and a box of food to camp for the weekend. Another possibility is to take in a retreat. Many Jewish and Christian communities offer marriage retreats at a reasonable cost, often subsidized by the sponsoring organization. If the price is still too steep, ask if they have a sliding scale payment plan. Some even offer scholarships.

Don't attribute every problem to being a blended family. Lots of the problems you struggle with are the very same ones confronting intact families. Try to develop some objectivity. Step back from the problem and ask yourself: What is the real cause of this situation? Is it truly because we are a blended family? Or is it just a part of life with a teenager (or a pre-adolescent, or a strong-willed child, or a kid with an inquiring mind, or two adults from different backgrounds)?

Train yourself to resist automatically assuming the worst. If your ex is late to pick up the kids, don't assume it's because he doesn't care about them or because she wants to irritate you. And don't pronounce that person hopelessly irresponsible. It's possible that he had a flat tire or that she received a long-distance telephone call from her sick mother just as she was leaving. Be generous enough to give the benefit of the doubt.

Don't turn issue issues into people issues. This is something we see happen over and over again. Let's say Sally dislikes her husband's ex-wife Christine. Since Sally dislikes Christine, she hates everything about Christine. So if Christine wants her child to play the saxophone, Sally is immediately against it. Sally's husband may think the saxophone is a great idea, but he doesn't want to fight with her over it.

More than once Bill has told Nancy, "Don't put me in the position of having to defend my ex-wife. Whatever the issue is, you and I will deal with it and leave her out of it."

Turn lose-lose situations into win-win situations. If you look at the conflicts in your relationships and determine in your heart that you *will win,* no matter what the cost, we can assure you that, in the end, you will lose. In relationships, one-upmanship is a killer; everyone loses. Instead of aiming for a victory, aim for a situation in which there is no loser.

How do you do this? We're glad you asked! It just so happens we have some tips for you:

1. Refuse to be vengeful.
2. Let your dealings with everyone be non-judgmental.
3. Understand the needs of your family.
4. Be aware of your finances and live within your means.
5. Refuse to compromise honesty.
6. Be sensitive to the feelings of others, even if those feelings seem to be silly.
7. Keep your goals reasonable.
8. Assure your children that both their parents love them, and that neither will abandon them. Also tell them the truth—there is no chance that you will reconcile with your ex.
9. Understand that *covert* messages about your ex-spouse ("If you need something, talk to your mother. She gets enough of my money") can harm your children just as much as *overt* messages ("Your mom bleeds me dry and doesn't even use the money for you").
10. Determine how you will best be able to communicate with your ex and with your spouse's ex, then start doing it.
11. Be willing to take another look at your position on an issue, even if you have a legal contract on your side. There is nothing to prevent you from being more generous and flexible than the law requires.
12. Put yourself in the other person's shoes.
13. Don't assume the worst in anyone.
14. Understand you can win a battle and lose the war.
15. Realize that you pay a high price for control.

16. Approach problems positively.
17. Focus on the future, not on the past.

WHEN YOU NEED EXTRA HELP

"My son says he hates my new spouse."

"Our 'his' children and 'her' children fight like cats and dogs. We're at our wit's end with them!"

"Despite my efforts, my ex-spouse will not be reasonable. There is no way the two of us can ever communicate civilly."

"My spouse's ex shouldn't be a parent at all. For the kids' good, we need to keep them away from her."

When problems persist, consult a counselor. Don't wait until things reach a crisis stage. Ask your doctor or pediatrician to refer you to an appropriate professional, or talk to friends or relatives who have had successful family counseling experiences.

AND NOW THE BENEFITS

When you are a member of a blended family, it's easy to look around you in judgment, anger, and blame. It's easy to pick out the negative things you see and to insist that the children are already damaged, that it is too late to do anything about it. But if you take this approach, you will be giving up the opportunity to experience the blessings unique to blended families. Before you surrender to the negative, consider these benefits:

There is a lot of extra support available to children in blended families. When Brent plays football, there are several kids and four caring adults in the stands cheering him on (half-siblings and stepsiblings, mother, stepfather, father, and stepmother—and sometimes two grandmas and a grandpa!). In our society, extended families are pretty much a thing of the past. But in many blended families, kids are surrounded by people who care deeply about them. What a special blessing this can be.

There are more adults to share the parenting responsibilities. Both Nick and Brent had to have fairly extensive orthodontic work done. We don't need to tell you how all those appointments interfered with our busy family schedule. But we ended up sharing the responsibility with each boy's other parent—not only the cost, but also the transportation to and from appointments.

Kids have more role models. Each person in your child's extended family has special strengths and unique abilities. When children have four adults actively involved in their lives—plus an assortment of grandparents and aunts and uncles—the number of positive role models greatly increases.

There will be more options open to your children. Two homes and four parents equal more options for the kids. For instance, if mom and dad are in different school districts, you can determine which house you want to use as the official school address, thereby choosing the best school for your child. We know a family who used mom's address for the children while they were in elementary school (they liked its back-to-basics approach), but for high school they used dad's district (it offered the students more choices).

Blended families have more resources available to them. Emily's health had been going downhill for years. When the doctor told her parents she would need a liver transplant, they fell apart. It was Sharon, her stepmother, who came forward and took charge. Sharon stayed by her stepdaughter's bed, conferred with the doctors and filled out endless papers and forms, and dealt with the insurance company. When Emily was released from the hospital, she moved in with her dad and Sharon, and Sharon became her nurse.

"No one else could do it," Sharon explained. "Emily's parents were so emotionally involved that they were next to dysfunctional. I love my stepdaughter, but I was removed enough to be objective."

Does your blended family have a chance to succeed? Absolutely! With effort and determination, you can be the exception to those depressing statistics.

Chapter 3

CHILDREN PULLED APART

How to Communicate Effectively with Your Ex So Your Kids Don't Suffer

Thousands of years ago, King Solomon of the Bible was presented with the ultimate parenting dilemma: Two women stood before him fighting over a baby boy.

"He's mine!" cried one. "Her baby died during the night. This one is mine!"

"No," insisted the other. "He's mine! It was *her* baby who died."

"Mine! Give him to me!" demanded the first woman.

"No, he's mine!" protested the other. "Give him to me!"

Back and forth they argued. Finally King Solomon ordered, "I'll solve this problem right now. Bring me a sword. You can each have half a baby!"

"Good," said the first woman. "Then neither of us will have him."

But the other woman cried, "Oh, please, no! Don't kill him! Give the baby to her!"

Wise King Solomon had his answer. A true mother would rather give her baby up than see the child destroyed.

Today, in our dealings with parents who insist on

pulling their children in two, we could use a bit of King Solomon's wisdom.

"My mom hates my dad and my dad hates my mom," a distressed ten-year-old said through her tears. "If I love my dad, my mom is mad at me. If I love my mom, my dad is mad. I want to love them both, but then they will both be mad at me."

"That's really sad," you may be saying. "I'll have to admit it could be my own child speaking. But the fact is, my ex divorced me, and that put my child at risk emotionally. It isn't a good situation, but nothing can be done about it."

Divorce causes children such emotional trauma that it scars them for life, right? Wrong. Research shows that what causes the most serious trauma and the deepest scars is *not* the divorce. It is the ongoing conflict between mom and dad, and that is something you can control. Your child does not have to be at risk. It's your choice.

When you tear down one parent, you are tearing down half the child. Even if the parent is abusive or lazy or a first-class jerk? Yes, even then. Whatever the parent's weaknesses, to tear him or her down destroys the goodness that also exists within that person.

"I know that sort of thing is hard on the kids," you may be saying, "so I make it a point not to run down my ex in front of them. Not that he deserves the kindness, mind you. But I keep my opinions to myself."

Are you sure? Running down your ex can be overt ("Your mother is a rat!") or covert ("I hope you have a wonderful time with your dad this weekend. Too bad you won't be with us. We're going to see the new exhibit at Universal Studios"). The implied message comes through loud and clear: "No matter how great your dad's plans for the weekend, he can't beat what we're doing."

Children learn from subtle messages who and what can be talked about and who and what should not be mentioned. "I wanted my dad to come to my sweet sixteen birthday party," Monique said. "But I knew it would upset my mom, so I didn't ask him. It's sad because I sure missed having him there."

Dottie took that burden off her daughter. "I made myself allow my ex-husband to come to the house and celebrate after my daughter's high school graduation. It was awfully hard to do, but it meant so much to her to have him there."

However hard it is, you can do it. After all, how many grad parties is your child going to have in her lifetime? How many college graduations? How many weddings? How many wedding receptions?

"Actually, the graduation party was a good first step," Dottie admitted. "My daughter had already informed me, 'When I get married, you and dad are going to have to be in the same place at the same time. You are going to have to deal with it, Mom. Grow up.' So, for my child's sake, I did."

"But I can't help how I feel about my ex!" you may say.

Fine. How you feel doesn't affect your children. What affects them is how you act. So act like a mature, caring adult. And while you are acting, perhaps you can work on letting go of some of your bitterness. We know of a well-educated, financially successful couple who were so angry and vindictive at the time of their divorce that we could do nothing but shake our heads and say, "Their poor kids are doomed!" Six years later we encountered those kids again. One was a habitual runaway, the second had been picked up for shoplifting, and the third was in jail on drug charges. If we had asked their parents back then, "Which is more important to you, your children or your hate for each other?" they would certainly have answered, "Our kids, of course!" But their behavior said just the opposite. They made the choice in order to hold on to their hate, and they sacrificed their children.

"I'LL JUST KEEP MY EX AWAY"

"My children won't have to choose between their parents," Marge declared. She tried to make sure of it by blocking them from any contact with Jim, their father. Her tactic was to charge him with sexual abuse. It cost Jim his equity in the house, but his lawyer finally convinced the judge that there was no basis for the charge. Marge didn't give up; she continued her fight, verbally, emotionally, and physically. One day she literally threw her body in front of Jim's car in the driveway to keep him from taking the children for the day. Finally, in frustration, Jim quit trying. Marge was jubilant. "Now, my children won't have to choose between us!"

You can speak in a positive way to your children about your ex-spouse, or you can speak negative words. The choice is yours. But understand that if you choose negativity, you are running the risk of causing your child the pain and anguish of being torn between the two of you.

The repercussions of parents intent on keeping their children to themselves don't stop when those children reach adulthood. When grown kids finally meet the parents they always heard criticized and maligned and discover they are not the evil jerks they were made out to be, there is almost always a backlash against the parents who made the negative comments. That is certainly what happened to Marge. Today, neither of her children is speaking to her. She is forced to stand on the sidelines and watch as her ex-husband enjoys the role of grandpa to the two little grandchildren she is barred from contacting.

Is it worth it? Ask Marge.

WHAT IF YOU AND YOUR EX DON'T COMMUNICATE?

"Well," you may say, "my ex and I don't talk at all. When the kids are picked up to go over there for a visit, I make myself scarce. I have a new family, and my ex has nothing to do with it. We have absolutely nothing to say to one another."

Why is that? Are you emotionally, verbally, or physically abusive to each other? Is there so much conflict between you that you cannot possibly hide it from the children? If so, it probably is best that you never be together in front of them. To avoid making a big issue of it, many people in such a situation are defining weekends as Friday after school through Monday morning. If the noncustodial parent can pick the child up from school on Friday and then drop her off at school on Monday morning, no contact between the parents is needed—and no explanation, either.

This can solve the problem of face-to-face confrontations, but you still need to have some communication with your child's other parent. It isn't realistic to think you can share your child's life yet never communicate about that child. We don't know how much you are realistically able to do with your ex-spouse. Some parents can do no more than write an informational note to each other—maybe only through their attorneys. Others are able to talk on the telephone. Still others can meet in a public place, such as a restaurant or perhaps even in one of their offices.

Which of these three basic levels of communication are you able to achieve?

WRITTEN CONTACT

If the two of you have not been able to communicate at all, you might want to begin by writing letters. The first tiny step would be to pass the letters through your attorneys. If this is where you are, work toward exchanging written communication directly, without the middle person.

A parenting notebook is one way to move toward this goal. A published version of such a notebook was developed by Steve Erickson and Marilyn Erickson McKnight, but it is something you can easily do on your own. All you need is a spiral notebook that can travel back and forth between the two of you with your oldest child. You can stick the notebook in a backpack, or, if your child is an infant, in the diaper bag.

Before you start your notebook, agree with your ex on two basic ground rules:

1. This is not a private diary of what goes on in either home. That would be totally inappropriate. Privacy boundaries are both healthy and desirable.
2. Everything that goes into the notebook must be positive in tone. If not now, someday your child will be able to read it.

Record anything in the notebook you feel will be helpful to the other parent, including:

- ❖ vital statistics of the children—dates of birth, social security numbers, and so forth
- ❖ the school schedule of each child
- ❖ names, addresses, and telephone numbers for club leaders, special friends, schools, and contact people
- ❖ important medical information: Name and telephone number of doctor and dentist, list of prescriptions, insurance coverage card number, list of allergies
- ❖ parental information—work address, schedule, emergency contact number
- ❖ an activity schedule for each child, including child care
- ❖ each child's daily routine, including medication and any special needs
- ❖ a record of accomplishments, special activities, upcoming events: field trips, school plays, soccer games, music recitals, church choir performances
- ❖ any changes at home: a new pet, remodeling that is going on, a best friend who has moved away. You might also address problems or concerns: fear of the dark, problems at school, talking back, bed wetting

♣ many parents attach folders and/or large envelopes to the notebook so that photographs, report cards, and drawings can be included

The notebook allows parents to communicate with each other without misunderstandings and undue stress.

If you and your ex-spouse are especially uncomfortable being in the same place at the same time, work out a plan for participating independently in such things as field trips, recitals, and back-to-school night. You might write in the book: "It will be very inconvenient for me to be at the soccer game this Saturday. If you can be there this week, I'll be sure to be there next week." Or: "I'm going to be at Christy's recital on Saturday afternoon and I hope you will also attend. It's important to her. Since I will be bringing her from my house and will have to arrive early and stay late, perhaps you could plan to celebrate with her after it's over. That way we will both be a part of this important event."

Do your best to be civil and flexible. When one parent is willing to set a higher standard, often the other follows.

"Good idea, but we don't need a parenting notebook," you might be saying. "My ex and I are able to talk to each other."

Great! But you may want to go the notebook route anyway. In most blended families, life is so crazy that you are sure to forget to tell your ex something important. Dad misses that big recital. Mom doesn't know about the conference with the teacher until it's too late to arrange her schedule. It's not intentional, it just happens because life is busy and you forget things. The notebook can keep information from getting lost in your heavy schedule.

TELEPHONE CONTACT

For parents who are able to talk with each other, we suggest setting up a regular monthly telephone parenting meeting. In our experience, Sunday night works well because everyone is back in town getting ready for the next week. It might be wise to schedule a time after the children are in bed—say, 10:00 p.m. or so. The two of you don't need to talk long. The purpose is simply to check in and see if anything special is going on with the kids—the school science fair project or homework in general—or if there are any behaviors you need to discuss. In other words, you're comparing notes. These conferences can be very positive for your children, because it lets them know that whatever the differences between you and your ex-spouse, when it comes to them, the two of you stand firmly side by side.

"I don't know," you may be saying. "I really don't think we can do that."

Don't decide until you try. Most parents are able to discipline themselves to talk about their children over the phone. If it truly isn't something you can do, see if you can get your ex to agree to a preliminary step. You might work with a mediator or a counselor for a while to help get the communication started. Or you might agree to call each other at prearranged times and leave messages on the answering machine. That way the information can be communicated without the two of you actually having to talk. Or you can fax if fax machines are easily accessed. Even kids' art can be faxed.

If verbal communication isn't possible today, work toward it. It's a worthwhile goal.

PERSONAL CONTACT

"I never thought I would be able to have personal contact with my ex-husband," Nancy says, "yet we ended up meeting every six weeks in a restaurant over coffee and it worked out just fine. In time we got so comfortable we began to meet at one or the other of our offices. One discussion over private school took place with both parents and both stepparents talking together in Bill's office."

Resist the temptation to play a power game when

your kids are at stake. As you talk over the welfare of the children you both care for so dearly, you will be surprised at how your trust level can increase.

When the trust level between parents is high, they might do some joint family events, such as birthday parties. But in-home parenting meetings are appropriate only after working long and hard to develop trust. The decision for Brent to begin living primarily with his dad was made in Nancy's ex-husband's family room, with his wife and Bill both there, over a plate of hors d'oeuvres. But that took place after years of good work on the part of both parents, the cooperation of the new spouses, and many parenting meetings in each other's offices.

Don't feel pressured to start out beyond your comfort level. Most people feel better about meeting in a public place. Some people will not feel physically safe anywhere else. Others feel they cannot trust themselves to stay in control if they are alone together. Still others simply don't feel comfortable in a private setting. Decide where your relationship with your ex is, then choose an appropriate place for your parenting meeting.

Letters, telephone contact, or in-person communication—if you try one and it doesn't work, take a step back and try again. But don't give up. Your child is too important.

MONEY TALKS

"It's hard to communicate when my ex tries so hard to buy my child's love . . . and is so successful at it!"

It's really tough when one family is able to provide a lot more than the other family can. The court takes the parents' income into consideration when support is set, but not the income of the new spouses. When Lorraine and Paul divorced, he was an accountant and she was a stay-at-home mother. Based on Paul's middle income and Lorraine's total lack of work experience or skills, the court put the weight of support for their two boys on Paul. Two years later, Paul married another stay-at-home mom and Lorraine married a financial wizard whose income was five times what Paul's was. Paul's support responsibilities remained the same, and so did Lorraine's. Lorraine and her new family jetted around the world; Paul paid child support. Lorraine took the kids to a great resort for winter vacation; Paul paid child support. Lorraine celebrated her oldest son's sixteenth birthday by surprising him with a new sports car; Paul struggled to buy him a pen set and pay child support. Fair? Maybe and maybe not, but that's how it is.

In such a situation, it's up to the more well-off parent to take steps toward evening out the playing field. If you are the more well-off parent, you might think about giving some of that support money back so your ex can take the kids on a vacation. Maybe it won't be the splashy ski resort you go to, but the kids would likely enjoy a camping trip with their other parent. To your lawyer, this might seem like an absolutely crazy thing to do because you are under no legal obligation to be so generous. But you're not thinking of legal, you're thinking of your child's psychological well-being. A lawyer's job is to think of the legal obligations and rights; your responsibility is much broader and more long-term.

Talk with your ex-spouse about money issues such as allowances for the children. It's very difficult if dad hands over a "generous" $25 a week and mom gives them a "measly" $5.

Talk also about gift-giving. By discussing before you buy for birthdays or Christmas, you won't end up duplicating gifts or giving the kids too much. Brent enjoys photography, but there is no reason for him to have an expensive camera at each home. It's nice for him and Nick to each have a nice suit, but they don't need one at each house.

Ellen's mom was in tough financial straits. She and

her new husband were struggling just to keep from going under. Ellen's dad, on the other hand, was prosperous and generous. He and his new wife showered Ellen with expensive clothes, stylish shoes, $200 sunglasses. Her room at her dad's house was decked out with a television and video player, a computer, a CD player and a stack of CDs. Every time Ellen came back from her dad's, she paraded in, proudly flaunting her "loot" and bragging about all her stuff at her other home. Ellen's two half-sisters would stand in the hallway watching jealously. "Why not us?" they demanded with resentment. "How come we don't get anything? Doesn't anyone love us?"

This is a tough situation to deal with. The best thing you can do is teach your children compassion and develop in them a sensitivity for the feelings of others. How? The most effective way is to model it yourself. Do you go out of your way to help those less fortunate than you? Do you refuse to look down on those who have less? Do you take advantage of situations that arise in school and the neighborhood to talk about the importance of being sensitive to others' feelings? In what specific ways, and through what actions, do your children see that sensitivity in you? An excellent way to put things in perspective is to volunteer as a family to pack Thanksgiving baskets or feed the homeless, or in some other way reach out to the less fortunate.

If you are struggling with an insensitive child, take her aside and talk to her. You might say something such as: "Ellen, I am so pleased you have all these things at your dad's house. I know you enjoy them. But we cannot give these things to your sisters. I don't think you realize how it affects them when you brag about your special things there and show off your new clothes each week. Please think about how you would feel if you were in their place."

If your child is younger—between seven and ten— you might ask, "Do you think you could not talk about all those things quite so much? You may not realize it, but it is hurting your sisters' feelings."

You say you don't think children are really capable of responding with sensitivity? Don't be so sure. Kids are constantly surprising us. Bragging and boasting usually turn off their friends, too. Unless your children learn at home to restrain themselves, they are in for a great deal of heartache.

WHEN ONE PARENT LIVES FAR AWAY

"My new husband has taken a job 600 miles away," a mom told her ex-husband.

"Tough. I'm still living here, and I want to be able to see my children."

"I have a right to stay with my husband," she insisted.

"I have rights, too, including the right to have regular contact with my kids."

His rights, her rights. Once again, the rights of the child get lost in the shuffle. If parents end up living far apart, they have a responsibility to work out a schedule that will keep their children in regular touch with both parents. They will need to schedule in blocks of time: summer, winter vacation, spring break. For instance, one parent may get ten weeks in the summer but very little in between.

"I hate it!" fourteen-year-old Adam said of his parents' schedule for him. "It isn't fair. Just to make things convenient for them, I have to leave my friends every summer and sit around looking like a geek in a town where I don't know anyone. I love my dad, but I want to be with my friends."

That's what Adam says, but his parents insist, "You're just being selfish. The issue here is not your friends."

So what is the issue? If it's to keep from pulling your children between you, look at the situation and ask yourself:

❖ Is what we are doing contributing to our child's overall well-being?
❖ What can I do to slant this situation in favor of my child?
❖ What can I do to help my child experience both parents without feeling torn between us?

Darlene and Tom are a good example. Darlene didn't want her ex-husband Tom to have their two-year-old son Joshua for the six-week block scheduled for him. She came to see Nancy, and Nancy stressed the importance of allowing the little boy to grow up knowing his father. She told her about the positive experiences her own son had shared with his father.

"Well, this is different," Darlene insisted. "Tom isn't even going to be taking care of Joshua while he's there. Tom's mother is!"

"That's fine," Nancy said. "That's his choice. Tell me, Darlene, is your resistance helping Joshua or hurting him?"

Darlene wasn't convinced, but she had little choice but to abide by the court's instructions. After the first week, Darlene came to see Nancy. "This shared parenting is great!" she exclaimed. "Tom's parents are having a wonderful time taking care of Josh, Tom is spending time with him in the evenings, and Josh is having the time of his life. And you know what? I just got a chance to go on a ski trip. For the first time since my son was born, I actually got away with friends!"

We have seen it happen again and again. Parents are so tied up in the issue of their divorce that they cannot move on to the bigger issue of parenting. Once they make a decision based on what is best for their children, they are amazed to discover that it is usually best for them as well. Similarly, when parents themselves are comfortable, their children tend to be comfortable as well. What could become a damaging, vicious cycle can instead be turned into a healthy lifestyle.

A SPECIAL PLACE FOR EACH CHILD

Regardless of how your children came into your family—whether by birth or marriage or adoption—reassure each one again and again that there is a special place in the family that only he or she can fill. Then prove it by your actions.

When our boys were young, we set aside Thursday night as family night. On this night, anybody could bring up anything for discussion. If one family member was having a problem with another family member, it could be talked through on family night and hopefully worked out. No one's concerns were less important than another's. It was a very positive time for all of us.

Another excellent way to reassure your children of the special place each holds in your family and in your heart is to control the things that come from your mouth day by day. Here are some positive, supportive things to say to your kids:

1. All of us love you—your parents and your stepparents.
2. Neither your mom nor your dad will leave you.
3. We will show you a schedule so you can see when you will be with Mom and when you will be with Dad.
4. You are an important part of both our families.
5. If you are thinking Mom and Dad will get back together, we want you to know it won't happen. Our families are different now, and it can never be the old way again.
6. I love spending time with you, and your other parent does, too.
7. I'm glad you are able to spend time with your other parent.
8. As you grow, schedules will change, but you

will always have both your mom and your
dad.

9. You have two homes, and both are equally
important.

10. Whatever differences your parents have, we
agree that we both love you.

YES, KIDS, YOU DO HAVE RIGHTS

"Everyone has rights but us!" Adam declared in disgust
after yet another war between his parents.

It may seem that way, but the fact is, kids do have
rights. Children have the right to

- ✤ develop an independent and meaningful relationship with each parent;
- ✤ respect and appreciate the personal difference of
each parent and each home, and never to have
these differences referred to as "better" or "worse";
- ✤ love parents and stepparents without feeling
guilty, pressured, or rejected;
- ✤ be loved, cared for, disciplined, and protected by
each parent;
- ✤ never have to take sides or to choose between
mom and dad;
- ✤ not hear mom and dad speak ill of each other
nor hear about the difficulties between them;
- ✤ see mom and dad courteous and respectful to
each other;
- ✤ express their feelings, even if those feelings are
anger or sadness or hurt or fear;
- ✤ be a child and not have to make adult decisions
or take on adult responsibilities;
- ✤ be given the most adequate economic support
both parents can provide;
- ✤ not have to participate in the destructive games
parents play to hurt and punish each other;

♣ never be used as a spy, a messenger, or a bar-
   gaining chip;
♣ never be thrust into the middle of their parents'
   battles;
♣ never, ever be pulled in two.

In the third chapter of the book of Ecclesiastes in the
Old Testament, Solomon wrote: "There is a time for every
purpose under heaven." He's right. There is a time to
hold tight, and a time to release your grip.

Are you a truly caring parent? Is your love stronger
than your desire to own and control and win? Are you
determined to preserve your children healthy and whole?
Then resolve that you will never make a Solomon baby of
your child.

Chapter 4

THE "WICKED" STEPPARENT

How to Defy the Label

Whe were two years into our life as stepparents when Nancy made this entry in her journal:

Being a stepparent is a no-win situation. Financially and emotionally I have all the responsibilities of a birth parent, but I have none of the legal rights. Right now, Bill is out of the country on business. Nick is supposed to be here with our family for three weeks, but his mom called and said she was keeping him with her. She knew that with Bill gone it would put me in a difficult spot, and it has. I don't know what to do. I feel uncomfortable about bothering Bill in Germany. Anyway, I ought to be able to handle these things myself. It's so frustrating!

It isn't easy being a stepparent. And to make matters worse, we have to endure the legacy left us by such childhood friends as Cinderella and Hansel and Gretel. For many people, "wicked" and "stepparent" just seem to go together.

We can't even imagine the pain that must come with a second divorce. How could we abide being completely cut off from the kids who are now ours in every way but blood? "What a warning to work diligently at a second marriage," Bill says. "For every time you blend families, you expand the group of people personally affected by a breakup."

"But I don't want to be a wicked stepparent," you may be saying. "I want to be loved. But what if . . .?" We know what you're thinking: What if, despite all you do, your stepchild doesn't like you? What if he never does feel comfortable talking to you? What if she never shows you any love or affection? What if your stepchild totally buys into the wicked stepparent myth and never even gives you a chance?

Well, then that's how it is. No one can force a child to accept a new parent. What you can do is love that child patiently and unconditionally. You can set down rules and guidelines that will help the child grow into a healthy, well-adjusted adult. When you have done the best you can, you can pray that, if nothing else, the child will come to respect you and appreciate you for your efforts.

THE INTRUDER

"My stepchildren's mom died when the kids were teenagers," Fran told us. "I'm thirteen years younger than she was, and that created a problem for the kids. At the very beginning I explained to them that their mom was special, and just like any special person, no one can ever replace her. Taking her place was not my purpose. My purpose was to finish the job their mother wasn't able to do. 'I'm going to make mistakes,' I told them. 'But I will promise you this: I will do the very best I can.'"

It wasn't easy for Fran and her husband. Her husband's youngest and Fran's eldest were both eleven-year-old girls—a situation Fran described as "a never-ending circus!" She was always finding herself caught between them. "Something would happen, and one girl would state, 'It's all right for me. She's my mom!'"

'Well, at least you've *got* a mom,' the other would shoot back.

'So, just because you don't have a mom, she should give you anything you want?'

'Well, now she's *my* mom, too!'

Someone always ended up angry, someone was always in tears.

It is even more likely that stepparents will be viewed as intruders when both parents are living and children feel emotionally pulled between their parents in two different homes. It's not uncommon for them to cry: *"Why, oh why can't my mom and dad get back together? Maybe if it weren't for this intruder, they would."*

IF ONLY THINGS WERE LIKE THEY USED TO BE

Even when a stepparent is loving and kind and patient, even when there is exemplary behavior between all the child's parents, that child may still wish mightily that mom and dad were back together loving one another once more. We can do everything right to keep from imposing anxiety on our children, yet they can turn around and create their own anxiety because they are unable to make their dearest wish come true.

When Lori and her husband were first married, he wasn't the residential parent for his two little children. Over and over again, the kids talked wistfully about wanting mommy and daddy to live together in the same house. From the very beginning, Lori and Don made it a point to be honest and direct. "It's not going to happen," they told the children. "We're together now. We love each other, and we are going to stay together, no matter what."

"We told the children both in words and by our actions that we would honor our commitment to ourselves, to them, and to God," Lori said.

The assurances didn't make the children stop wishing. It wasn't anything against Lori. The children were grieving their own loss. "I knew their hearts were saying, 'I love everybody, and I feel good about everybody. So why can't we all be together?'" Lori did her best to remain patient and understanding, yet she was firm in her resolve. Over time, the children's need to have everyone under one roof slowly began to dissipate.

If your children can't let go of their wish to see mom and dad back together, follow Lori's example. Tell them the truth. Leave no doubt about the fact that the family has changed forever. ("Anne is my wife now. We are a family, and you are an important part of it. Your mother and I will never get back together, but neither of us will ever stop loving you.")

CHILDREN IN PAIN

At the age of nineteen, Marilyn's youngest daughter is just now telling her mother how angry she was about the divorce nine years before. "I never had any idea that was bothering her," Marilyn said. "Sure, she had been acting out, but I thought it was just her age."

"I just get angry, I can't help it," eight-year-old Katie said. "Things happen that make me so mad."

"I liked it better when it was just Mom and me," said Justin. "Now there is him, too, and his two girls. Mom says they are my sisters, but they aren't. I *hate* them!"

"I'm good because I don't argue and fight," Matthew said. "My mom always says, 'You're doing so good.' But I worry a lot. I'm not really sure what is happening, so I just be quiet."

Your kids are struggling, feeling pulled between the people they care about the most. "But I ask my children if anything is bothering them," you may say. Good for you. And yet, what are your kids going to say? Think of it from their perspective. Their issue is simple: *I want to be loved. I want to do what is going to make me accepted. I want to know I'm a worthwhile person.* What will get them these things? Probably the answers: "I'm okay. Everything's fine. Don't worry about me."

With all the changes and adjustments going on in your child's life, it is unrealistic to think there won't be problems. Whether he shows it or not, your child is undergoing a difficult time.

"My stepmother was a good mom," Tricia said. "She had time to do everything. She was the coach for my soccer team and the referee for my brother's basketball team. She was room mother for me and den mother for my little brother's scout troop. She would always bake cookies for the bake sales and she would go on field trips with us. But then she and my dad got a divorce and she was gone. I miss her a lot."

Divorce presents children with a whole series of significant losses. What adults view as necessary change, children perceive as a sad, frightening event. To a child, divorce means losing home, family, friends, loving parents who care about each other, pets, financial security, relationships with extended family, familiar schools, sports activities, and their familiar daily routine. Children often feel uprooted and abandoned. Respect your child's pain by eliminating as many changes and losses as you possibly can.

One mother said, "Everything is hard right now, but I can handle it. That is, I can handle everything except my little daughter's incessant whining. It's driving me crazy! If she would give me a break and stop the whining, everything would be okay."

That's not going to happen, mom. You aren't going to be able to wish the difficulties away. We know it makes it harder on you, but you need to listen to your whining child. Find out what is behind the behavior. Only when you determine where your child is emotionally can you put yourself into a position to help.

"You obviously don't know my child," you may be saying. "He is so rebellious that no one can get along with him."

Try to determine what is behind that rebellion. Your son is fuming about his "unfair" teacher and refusing to go back to school? Your daughter can't get along with the other children on the playground? Sit down with your child and listen to the complaint. You may be surprised at what you hear.

When Daniel came home with a note from his teacher saying he was having problems on the playground, his mother gave him a sound scolding. Daniel yelled, "I hate school!" then he stomped off to his room and slammed the door shut after him. That's when Daniel's mother decided she had better pay closer attention both to her son's words and to his actions. She went to school and talked to his teacher. What she discovered was that the kids were making fun of Daniel's slight stammer. When he responded by crying, they refused to play with him. Already feeling rejected at home, Daniel felt doubly rejected at school. No wonder he hated it.

You say you're struggling with your own dilemmas and problems? You say you're under a great deal of stress yourself? That you're far too pressured and rushed to sit and listen to the kids' problems? We know. We've been there. But you need to step outside your own feelings and gather the energy to make the time. Your children's welfare is at stake.

Many children are not able to verbalize their feelings. They often don't even *know* what their feelings are. And even if they do, they don't have the vocabulary to describe their pain and confusion. All they know is that they feel terrible. So they act out what they are unable to say— grades plummet, behavior changes, they lash out at those close to them. But since children don't always direct their angry actions toward the appropriate person, parents are confused, frustrated, and hurt. It's especially hard on step-parents.

A PARENT WITH NO LEGAL RIGHTS

Jamie was just two when her mom married Mike. The little girl had never known her birth father, and he had never shown the least bit of interest in her. Although Mike couldn't legally adopt Jamie, she could never remember when he wasn't her daddy. Two days after her twelfth birthday, Jamie was informed that her mom and dad were getting a divorce. She felt shattered.

"From here on out, it's just you and me," Jamie's mom told her daughter. "We don't need anyone else."

"But what about Dad?" Jamie protested. "I want to see him."

"He's not your real father, Jamie," her mom said sternly. "I told him he wouldn't be able to see you any more. Put him out of your mind."

"You can't do that!" Jamie cried. "I'm not the one getting the divorce!"

Unfortunately, like it or not, she was. Mike had absolutely no legal rights to participate further in Jamie's life.

Divorce isn't the only thing that can cut stepparents off from their stepchildren, as Tina learned after her husband's car was hit head-on and he was instantly killed. The day after the funeral, she received a letter from her stepchildren's mother informing her that she was to have no more contact with the children she had shared her life with for five years.

"It was heartbreak on top of heartbreak," Tina said through her tears. "Now I have nothing. How could their mother be so cruel?"

"It isn't fair!" stepparents all across the country are crying. No, in individual cases it isn't fair. But legally, with the number of divorces and remarriages and the resulting family entanglements, it would be terribly complicated for the courts to step in and attempt to spell out all who might have legal standing under what circumstances, and which rights would be fair to whom. That could be disastrous to our court system. And there's another concern: With rights come responsibility. Should stepparents also be responsible for the support of their stepchildren? How about for their college finances or their medical costs? How about for long-term care in the case of a disability?

Here is our suggestion: Don't focus on the legal system, with all its limitations and frustrations. Once again, try to see the situation through your children's eyes. Be respectful of what is important to them. Does your ex have children who are no relation to you, but who are important to your child? Consider inviting them to your child's birthday party. Is something special going on at the other house during time the child is scheduled to be with you? Rearrange the schedule so your child won't miss out.

Our family doesn't celebrate Halloween, but Brent's other family does. Taking his little brother trick-or-treating is something he enjoys very much. It would be unfair of us to say, "But October 31 is Brent's night with us!" We look from Brent's perspective and make sure he gets that special time to spend with his little brother.

Many people get caught up in a report card sort of mentality. "I gave in last time," they say, "so you have to give in this time." Keeping score is a totally inappropriate approach to a child's life. Nick has a stepbrother and half-sisters on our side, but only his mother on the other side. There's no way things can ever be even between the two families.

"Well, I have needs, too," you may be saying.

Of course you do. We all do. But, once again, we need to focus on our children's needs. And there is a good side to this situation. Where there is give, there is also take. You're going to want the same type of considerations for your own child's birthday or your upcoming family reunion. If you have been generous and flexible, the other family is likely to be the same way with you.

WHEN THE "WICKED" EPITHET APPLIES

"Okay, so I sometimes yell at my stepkids. But they push and push until they drive me absolutely crazy."

"I have to admit I sometimes explode and call my wife's ex a jerk in front of the kids. But the fact is, he is a jerk. If he wants to be respected by me or the kids, he has to be respectable."

Your stepkids may well drive you crazy. And your spouse's ex may indeed be an irresponsible jerk. But please, don't fall into the trap of trying to justify your sins by the misdeeds of others.

Mitchell, a prominent physician and a deacon in his church, went to his children's school to pick them up for the weekend. To his amazement, a teacher who saw him coming shoved the kids into her car and roared off down the street. He was dumbfounded. "I thought my children were being kidnapped!" he told us.

When Mitchell hurried to the school office to get help, everyone treated him as though he were some sort of monster. The principal blocked the doorway and ordered, "Leave now or we'll call the police!"

Only later did Mitchell learn that his ex-wife and her husband had gone to school that morning and informed the principal that they suspected Mitchell of sexually abusing the children. Then the two called the church where Mitchell worshiped and repeated the accusations. Even though there was no evidence to back the charges, everyone reacted as though it were fact.

Mitchell had plenty to say to his children about their mother and the "nut" she was married to. A huge fight between the two families ensued, one of the nastiest we have ever witnessed.

Like Mitchell, Nina felt justified in lashing out at the

person she considered the guilty party in the family. "Nothing I could say about my husband's ex-wife would be too bad," Nina stated. "She betrayed him and his family. If it weren't for her repeated affairs, they would still be together and I wouldn't be raising her children."

Nina doesn't feel the least bit hesitant to tell her stepchildren, "Your mother was a bad mother. She left you. She doesn't love your dad, and she doesn't love you. I'm your mother now."

Nina truly believes she is making herself a hero to her stepchildren. In reality, she is doing just the opposite.

OTHER NAMES AND LABELS

Byron and his twelve-year-old son had been living together for a long time, just the two of them, when Marsha entered their lives. "I knew I wasn't just marrying the man," Marsha said. "I was marrying man, child, and ex—the whole package."

When Marsha and Byron were engaged, Byron Jr. didn't know what to call this new woman. Picking up on his uneasiness, Marsha told the boy, "Let's not make this an issue. You call me Marsha for as long as you feel comfortable. If you ever get to a point where you want to call me Mom, that would be great, too. But it's no big deal."

That was it. No issue. For the first year, Byron Jr. called her Marsha. Then suddenly one day it was *Mom*. No questions asked, no explanations given. From then on, Marsha was *Mom* and his birth mother was *Mother*.

Marsha, a counselor to adoptive parents, does not like the term *stepmother*. "It throws an automatic wall between you," she says. "How you introduce your children helps to frame the whole family unit for them. They're getting their understanding mostly from what they see you believe. I wouldn't want Byron to introduce Byron Jr. as my stepson, and I would never refer to him that way." How does she introduce him? "I say, 'This is my son, Byron.'"

Names and labels are important issues for blended families. The matter is complicated because what is comfortable for the children may not be comfortable for the adults, and the other way around. Marsha's approach worked well in her family. In other families, another approach may work better.

"My girls would never introduce James as their dad," said Dottie. "It always hurt me that they never accepted him as their dad, but that's how it was."

James agreed. "I'm their stepfather. That's how they feel, and I'm all right with it."

The fact is, most of us are uncomfortable using the same endearing term to refer to two people. "My mother died when I was seventeen," Marilyn said. "A couple years later, when my father remarried, we kids were all told to call his new wife *Mother*. I couldn't do it. I always referred to her as Mom; my birth mother would always be *Mother* to me."

Such a simple matter as a label can drive a wedge between child and stepparent that can never be removed. Do whatever works in your own family and accept your stepchildren's terms for you graciously. Marsha's advice was excellent: Take the issue out of it. Talk about it unemotionally.

Sometimes even this is difficult. If you approach a thirteen-year-old who has already let you know in no uncertain terms she wants nothing to do with her mother's new husband, and ask, "What do you want to call him, dear?" you can expect fireworks. She will probably shoot back, "What do you *think* I want to call him?" To even suggest she call him Dad would mean all-out war.

You say being called by your first name feels cold and impersonal? You say you long to be called Mom or Dad? You say if you could just get the child started with the label you prefer, he would get used to it and in time feel closer to you?

We say, let it go. In our experience, most children call their stepparents by their first names. It generally seems more comfortable for the child, at least at first. Generally, but not always.

"When Michelle came to live with us, she was fifteen years old and had never really had a dad," Bill recalls. "I asked her what she wanted to call me and she said, *Dad*. That was fine. If she had felt more comfortable calling me *Bill*, that would have been all right, too. Brent calls me *Bill* and Nick calls Nancy, *Nancy*, but they each have two active birth parents in their lives. It makes sense they would be less likely to say *Dad* or *Mom* to us. It could feel like a betrayal to their own parents."

What's in a name? Choose to see only one thing—an acceptance of you as part of your stepchild's life.

WHEN STEPPARENTS DO BEST

"My ex-wife Eileen abused our children," Gary said. "One day while I was at work she broke our two-year-old daughter's arm and blackened our four-year-old son's eyes. She was jailed, we got a divorce, and I was given custody of the children. We had no contact with her at all."

When Eileen's sentence was served, she fully expected to take up where she left off as her children's mother. Gary had other ideas. "I insisted the kids never be alone with her. She could see them, but only if someone else was there." The judge agreed. Eileen was furious.

That's when Suzanne entered the picture. "She was wonderful to the kids," Gary said. "That made Eileen jealous and more angry than ever. She took every opportunity to fill their heads with *wicked stepmother* stuff."

Suzanne refused to accept it. "The problem wasn't the kids, it was their mother," she said. "So I went to work on her. I told her she would always be their mom, but that my role was to mother them on a day-to-day basis. I asked her to help their father and me do the very best for the kids we possibly could."

What Suzanne achieved could be best described as an uneasy truce. Eileen keeps careful watch for anything she can term a "parenting violation." Yet Suzanne has been successful. She acted in her stepchildren's best interest, and in so doing escaped the *wicked* label.

You may say, "A good way to keep the children's best interest in mind would be to let them help make family decisions that are going to affect them, right?"

Not necessarily. If you give children a say in big decisions ("I won't marry her unless you agree," "Do you think we should have a new baby?" "Should mom get a full-time job or not?"), you are forcing them to shoulder some awfully big responsibilities. What if they are against the marriage, and you end up alone and totally miserable? What if they say, "No more children in this family!" and you always regret never having a child together? What if they say, "We sure could use the extra money. Get a job, Mom," and you end up miserable, stuck in a job you hate. As time goes on, you are going to feel resentful and they are going to feel responsible for what comes from their decisions.

Certainly, the older a child is, the more important it is to get his or her input into family matters. When you are considering buying a new house, for instance, you wouldn't ask the advice of a three-year-old, but you would likely consult a sixteen-year-old. But whether the child is three or sixteen, only ask for input, ideas, and opinions. The final decision should be up to you and your spouse.

"I encounter this all the time," Nancy says. "Parents will tell their kids, 'When you're twelve, you can decide where you want to live.' In a few states, that's the law. Even if that's the case, why would you give an important decision like that to a child? It is totally inappropriate."

FROM "WICKED" TO "SUPER"

"I do not want to be a wicked stepparent," you may be insisting. "I love my stepchildren, and I truly do want what is best for them. Do you have specific suggestions for me?"

We're glad you asked! Here are some techniques we have seen work over and over again:

Refuse to compete. There is room in a child's heart for everyone—mother, father, stepparents, siblings, step-brothers and stepsisters, grandparents, and many more. Do your best to fill your place in the child's life and don't begrudge anyone else his or her place.

"I had no intention of competing with my stepchildren's dead mother," Fran said. "I wanted to encourage them to keep the memory of their mom alive. I got a photo album for each of the children and put pictures of the family—including their mother—in it. We talked about her frequently. I wanted the children to know that she was a good person who did a lot of good things—and also a few bad things. I wanted them to know I, too, would make some really good decisions and do some great things, but I would also make mistakes and bad choices. That's what life is all about. It didn't have to be her or me, there was room for both of us."

Put an emphasis on communication. It is impossible to overemphasize the importance of communicating. Whatever the concern, whether tiny or huge, nothing can be settled if it isn't brought out into the open.

Byron Sr.'s own parents were divorced after all their children were grown and gone from home. In time, his mother remarried. "I didn't have much of a relationship with my dad," Byron recalled, "and even though I was twenty-three years old when my mother remarried, I really longed for a father figure. I liked my mom's new husband a lot, and whenever I was at their house I would call him Dad. Then one day my mother told me he had told her it made him uncomfortable, that he wanted me to call him by his first name instead. I did, but after that I always felt uneasy around him. I couldn't stop wondering why he didn't want to be my dad. Even more, I couldn't figure out why he didn't talk directly to me. I never found out because I never asked him."

Accept that your way is not the only way. People are different. Just because your spouse, or your ex, or your spouse's ex, or your kids or stepkids don't do things your way doesn't mean that person is wrong. Recognize that there are different ways of looking at things, and be willing to listen to the ideas of others.

Practice what you preach. Whether in an intact family, blended family, adopted family, test-tube family, or any other type of family, every parent is going to have weak points and strong points. What you do will speak far more loudly to your children than what you say to them. By watching you work out difficult situations, they learn to work out their own tough situations. By watching your flexibility, they learn to be flexible. By watching you set aside your own best interest for them, they learn to act out of love.

Join a support group. When things are tough and you feel you are struggling alone, consider the benefits of meeting with others who share your situation. Look for a support group that is positive, affirming, and that encourages you to explore your options. Together, with others who are struggling through similar issues, you can share experiences, insights, and techniques.

Look for support groups in your church or synagogue. Many community colleges, and some elementary and high schools, offer parenting classes that have a special application to blended families. Another possibility is your local mental health or social service center. A lot of places have resource directories available through government agencies, such as the Social Services or Health Department.

When such a group gets together, emotions can run high. Things can get out of hand and wounds can be reopened. That's why it's important to have someone in charge who is trained in facilitating group work. That person will be able to pull the group back together and to assist toward healing.

Many states are now requiring parents to attend children of divorce classes. Most of these are open to stepparents and should be attended by all the caring adults in a child's family.

Love the kids. Nothing can compete with the power of love and acceptance. It is amazing how quickly you can assimilate into your family a child who wasn't born to you. When our Joanna arrived as a needy little four-year-old, we had no idea what we were getting into. But despite the many problems, she wasn't with us two days before we felt she was 100 percent our child. It also happens with stepkids. Realistically, the assimilation is probably slower when the child has another parent, because you have to deal with the realities of that other person. But with time and patience, your family can become one unit.

Be a peacemaker in your home. Your stepchildren should consider home a haven, a place where they can relax and be accepted for who they are. You can be a peacemaker for them if you begin by making peace within yourself.

A TRUE PARENT

Parenting is a challenge for people who conceive and bear children. As stepparents we assume our challenges are totally different and twice as insane. That's what we get for assuming.

Our source for love isn't our kids' behavior, their physical appearance, or the honors they receive. We don't love them because they love us first, nor because they make us look good. We love them because of who they are: special individuals made by God. And the fact that they were not born to us doesn't make them any less special.

When we talk about blended families, we speak of stepparents and stepchildren for the purpose of sorting out who is who. But in actual life, we are just parents and children. Taking out the "step" can change the authority figure. There will be no reason to think, "Well, that's just my *step*child, so the main responsibility doesn't lie with me." Once you marry that child's parent, you become a parent yourself.

Please know and believe that you are an important part of that child's life. Often when kids hit adolescence, they won't talk about important or touchy topics with their parents. Your being there for the child can carry him or her over traumatic and treacherous situations.

"I bore that 'wicked stepmother' label for many years, but it was okay because I knew what I was doing was right," Fran told us. "I held tightly some advice the Bible gives: 'Train up a child in the way he should go and when he is old he will not depart from it.' It was absolutely true. Every one of those six kids have embraced things that were taught them by me, the wicked stepmother!"

Stepparent, start immediately to develop a parenting plan with your spouse. Stick together and hold fast to that plan. If you stumble and fall, pick yourself up, get back to the plan, and move forward. If the kids argue and complain, listen to them, then move on with your plan. They are just kids, and they can't be expected to understand everything. When you are successful, go out and celebrate. When you are hurt and discouraged, go out and celebrate. It is all part of the parenting process, and simply sticking together and hanging on is great success.

There may be times when things will seem downright hopeless. Whatever you do, and however hard you try, the kids may still brand you "mean" or "wicked."

However deeply you love them, they may yell, "You aren't my parent! I hate you!" When that happens, repeat to yourself, "This, too, shall pass." You may cry a lot. You may develop calluses on your knees from spending so much time praying. But you *will* get through it.

Children say cruel and hurtful things because they are hurt and confused. They just don't know how to handle their pain. Perhaps you can find comfort in the fact that kids often lash out at the one who is most actively reaching toward them. Often they pick the safest person to attack: the one they can depend on to be their port in the storm, the one who will be there for them no matter what they say and do and love them unconditionally.

"Wicked stepparent" is only a label. It is *only a label.* The time will come when your stepkids will realize that the person who carried that label was the one who was always there for them. He was the one who got up in the middle of the night and went to pick them up when they got stranded at the concert. She was the one who went out and fixed their flat tire. The wicked stepparent was the one who was consistent, the one who made allowances for their immaturity, the one who felt the pain of their verbal attacks but refused to take it personally.

"My husband finally got his stepparenting reward," Helene told us. "Last week, my sixteen-year-old son thanked him for everything he had done and put up with over the years. Then he hugged his stepfather and said, 'I love you, Dad. In my heart, you are my true father.'"

Yes, stepparent, you too are a true parent.

Chapter 5

EXTENDED FAMILY

Help or Hindrance?

When fifteen-year-old Annette Brownlee and her eighteen-year-old boyfriend Scott Sullivan told Annette's parents she was pregnant, her father responded: "You'll get married immediately!"

"Yes," her mother chimed in. "You can live with us until you are on your feet, and we will help you raise the baby."

When Scott and Annette told the Sullivans the plan, they were every bit as adamant: "You will do nothing of the sort! You won't marry until you are both through school."

The families fought, Annette cried, and Scott grew thoroughly frustrated. In the end, the couple didn't marry. But they did continue to date, and Scott was present when little David was born. Scott stayed in school and held down a job, yet he continued to see Annette and David regularly.

Just before David's second birthday, Annette was on her way to pick Scott up from work when a pickup truck crossed the center line and hit her car head-on. Annette died instantly.

Scott was still in shock when he received notice that Annette's parents had filed an action to adopt little David. "Why shouldn't we get him?" the Brownlees reasoned. "Scott didn't marry Annette, and he never paid child support. David has always lived with us. So let's just make it legal." Sure, Scott had bought diapers and baby food, and he had always been there for emotional support and had spent time with the child regularly. But the Brownlees didn't consider that *real* child support.

Scott was appalled. "They want to cut me out of my son's life!" he cried to his lawyer, who happened to be Nancy. "Don't I have any rights at all?"

Here were three people who truly loved and cared about a little boy and honestly wanted what was best for him. Nancy immediately filed a motion for mediation.

The day before the trial was to begin, and unbeknownst to the court, Scott and the Brownlees mediated a contact schedule for the nonprevailing party. That way, however the trial turned out, neither side would be totally cut off from David.

When they came before the judge, Annette's mother stubbornly refused to acknowledge that Scott had any right at all to raise his child. "This is a terrible situation," the judge said to the Brownlees' lawyer. "This child is going to be the loser here. I have listened to Mrs. Palmer's cross-examination of Mrs. Brownlee, and I'm telling you, you don't have abandonment here. Go out and see if you can't work something out."

Because the groundwork had already been laid in mediation, they were able to work out a shared parenting agreement where Mrs. Brownlee mothered David but Scott was the boy's primary residential parent. To make the transition as easy on David as possible, Scott slept on the Brownlees' sofa every night until the boy got used to being with him full-time.

The arrangement worked well until two years later when Scott got married. Grandma Brownlee was used to being David's mother. Now she had to deal with a step-mother, and she didn't like it one bit. So Scott and the Brownlees went back to mediation, just as a divorced couple might do. They worked out a schedule where David lived with his grandparents one week a month, spent time with them in the summer, and was with them on alternating holidays.

"Why are you doing this?" Scott's wife asked him. "David is *your* son. Legally you don't owe those people anything. Why are you so generous?"

"Because," Scott explained, "David's grandparents are important to him. I want to do what's best for my son."

The Brownlees may have never understood how fortunate they were.

EXTENDED FAMILY: HELP OR HINDRANCE?

Grandparents and other friends and family members can be incredibly positive and supportive to a blended family, or they can be detrimental and divisive. They care deeply, but it's easy for people who care to let their prejudices and opinions override their better judgment. Jessica's grandparents are a good example.

Little Jessica bounced into her house, home from her afternoon with her grandparents. "You know what Grandma says?" Jessica asked her mother between bites of chocolate chip cookie. "She says Dad is a first-class loser."

It so happened that Jessica's mother agreed with Grandma's assessment. Now she had a choice. She could express her agreement, either in words or by a well-timed snicker. Or she could ignore the comment and let the little girl come to her own conclusion. Or she could explain to Jessica that although people may have different opinions, it is not all right to call one another names. She could also determine to call Grandma immediately and explain that instead of helping, she was hurting Jessica by expressing such judgments to the child.

Many of us have our own friend-and-family support group. It's great to have those people firmly in our corner, cheering us along and encouraging us. But because they love us, they cannot see the whole situation clearly and objectively.

"My mother told me that until my stepfather's death, he firmly believed my ex-husband was 100 percent responsible for our divorce," Nancy says. "If I had known that while he was still alive, I would have corrected this huge misconception. I would have sat him down and told him divorces are never totally the fault of one person."

In mediation, Nancy is often able to bring parents to a point where they will agree to tell their own parents, friends, and supporters to refrain from making disparaging remarks about the other person. "They agree to let those people know that even though the remarks are made out of love and caring, the words do harm to the children's self-esteem and must end immediately."

That's the negative side. There is also a positive side. These special people can be, and often are, a wonderful influence on a blended family. Jesse and Teresa Castillo and their five children are a military family. When Jesse was sent to Okinawa for a year, his parents stepped forward and did their best to fill the hole in the family. Grandpa filled in as surrogate father for the children, always ready to pick up someone from soccer practice or music lessons or after-school activities. And he was always on hand to help Teresa with house repairs and car upkeep. Grandma willingly watched the children so Teresa could have a break, and she baked cookies, vacuumed the house, and generally made herself useful.

The grandparents also encouraged the cash-strapped family to talk on the telephone long-distance once a week—at their expense. And they regularly took pictures of the children and sent them along to Jesse in their frequent letters.

"We have a stake in this family," they explained. "We want to do everything we can to keep their relationships strong during this difficult time."

Unfortunately, Brownlee-type grandparents are more common than Castillo-type grandparents. Too often, grandparents want to take over the role they think has been abandoned by one of the parents. Or they feel totally justified in freely giving their assessment of the person they think is at fault in the domestic problems. This sends a terrible message to the kids.

"I'm afraid we weren't great parents," one grandmother confessed. "We were young and inexperienced when we had our family. But things are different now. We have matured and learned from our mistakes. We are the best people to raise our grandchildren." It makes sense to them, so they are ready to take over despite the wishes of the children's parents.

And what of the grandchildren who are not related to their grandparents by birth? What of those who were adopted or who entered the family by marriage? Our plea to those grandparents is this: Treat those grandchildren no differently than you treat your biological grandchildren. Remember their birthdays, Christmas, and other special occasions in the same way. They need your love and support every bit as much.

Our extended families were great. Bill's family was as kind and generous and accepting as they could be. Never throughout the blending process did they say anything negative. Nancy's divorce was hard on her family, yet they, too, were supportive. Not everyone is so fortunate.

"Out of my nine brothers and sisters, my divorce was the first," Ruth said. "In fact, it was the first divorce ever in our family, on either side. Aunts, uncles, grandparents—we could count over fifty marriages, and not one divorce among them. Needless to say, mine was a horrible blow to the entire family. I was a failure. To make it worse, I didn't keep my children with me. No one cared that my ex and I talked over all the ramifications and felt it was best for the kids to stay with him. Everyone looked at me living alone in a small apartment while my ex-husband and children stayed in the family home, and they whispered that I must be an alcoholic, or a child abuser, or maybe I was headed for a mental institution. All they saw in me was a woman who couldn't be a successful wife or even a successful parent. It's a family stigma I carry to this day."

Did Ruth try to explain to them?

"No," she said. "They didn't care. Why waste my time and theirs?"

Your extended family can provide wonderful allies for your blended family. Encourage them by letting them know what you need from them. Be willing to talk so they will have a chance of understanding your position. But if they insist on pulling you down, move away and draw your power from your new family.

GRANDPARENTS AND THE LAW

The role of grandparent is a wonderful and important and beautiful one. But it is a different role from that of parent.

"We are important, and we have rights!" is the cry of grandparents across the country.

That is certainly true. Grandparents *are* important, as are aunts and uncles and cousins and friends. But grandparents are not parents, and they do not have parental rights.

The Brownlees, Annette's parents and David's grandparents, found it unbelievable that Scott actually had the power to cut them out of David's life. "All I can say is it's a good thing Scott's cooperating with us," Mr. Brownlee stated. "If he didn't, we would sue him."

That's not an uncommon action for grandparents to

take. They feel strongly about their positions, and compared to their kids, they have the time and money to do it. But the court system is the worst place to deal with family disputes. How much better to work out problems through counseling or mediation than through a lawsuit.

"All we want is our fair share of our grandchildren's lives," many grandparents proclaim.

When grandparents first started vying for rights, their idea was simply to get a piece of the pie: If the kids have eleven weeks of vacation in the summer, dad would get four, mom would get four, and grandparents would get three. That's not what has happened. While the courts do recognize that grandparents have rights, those rights are not the same ones afforded parents. And to be honest, we think this is appropriate. Kids' lives are already divided up enough. Mom can share her contact time with her parents, and dad can share his with his parents.

UNMARRIED PARENTS AND THE LAW

"It would have been different if Scott had married Annette," the Brownlees insisted. "Then he really would have had a right to David. But they *weren't* married, and that changes everything."

Actually, it doesn't. And why should it? Little David still has the same need for a father in his life and for emotional and financial support from that father. Not only is it the right thing for a child, it is the law in most states. Yet the general public still assumes that since it is the mother who bears the child, she is the one who calls the shots. That is absolutely wrong.

"What?" many unmarried women exclaim. "You mean he actually can have a say in what name goes on the birth certificate (decide how the baby is raised, determine where the baby will live, share in the parenting)?"

He certainly can. Many dads want to parent these days, and many more are capable of doing so. In fact, we are seeing more and more men who were themselves raised in households where fathers had primary parenting roles.

"Wait!" a mother may say. "I won't accept child support. Then he won't have any rights to the baby, right?"

Wrong.

"But I'm not allowing him to help make decisions about the baby's life."

Makes no difference what you allow. Those things don't affect the rights of the child's father. That's a fact in most every state.

"But that's not fair!"

Actually, it is fair. Understand that we are not actually talking about the *father's* rights, just as we are not actually talking about the *mother's* rights. What we are talking about is the right of a child to have both parents involved in his or her life.

IF YOU CAN'T SAY SOMETHING NICE . . .

"I understand about children having a right to both their parents, but I don't know about trying to control comments from grandparents or other relatives and friends," you may be saying. "It's a lot to expect for those people to watch every single thing they say. They love me, and they want to champion me."

True. But the most important element here is the underlying attitude of the people close to your children. Someone can say, "She is a wonderful person" in a way that makes it a lovely compliment or with a sarcastic twist that makes it a mockery. A grandparent can choose to dwell on the negatives of her ex-son-in-law, or she can pull out the positives. It all depends on the attitude.

Encourage the people in your and your children's lives to look honestly at their motives. Encourage them to ask: What can I do in a positive way for this family? How can I build each person up? How can I make the blended family stronger? If it is absolutely too hard for Grandma to say something positive about her ex-daughter-in-law, ask her to respect your wishes and your child's best interest, and to say nothing at all.

CAUGHT IN THE MIDDLE

Of course it is not always that other person who does the damage. Sometimes that person is simply caught in the middle.

A wealthy blended family employed Lucie as their nanny. It was a good move because the mother and her ex-husband refused to communicate with each other in any way. So it was Lucie's job to go between the homes with the children and keep things on track. It worked well while the children were young. But because Lucie was the constant in their lives, she was the one they increasingly looked to for mothering. In time, she took on the role of a loving, nurturing parent. Both mom and dad were relegated to the position of interested bystanders, usually responding to the kids' requests with, "We'll have to see what Nanny says."

We have seen the same thing happen with other caring people—aunts, baby-sitters, teachers, and certainly grandparents.

Schools hate being caught in the middle of disputing parents who demand that the school take sides. We know of stepsiblings who were attending a local private school when a dispute arose among their various parents and stepparents. Everyone insisted to the school personnel, "I'm right! You have a responsibility to back me up and help me. If you don't, you will be held responsible for whatever happens."

When one parent charges the other with physical or sexual abuse, the school has to do its best to protect the children. That's what the teacher who rushed Mitchell's children into her car and roared off when he came to pick them up thought she was doing. But the action astounded and terrified him. In the end, Mitchell was angry at the school, the school was angry at the mother who had made the groundless charges, and the kids—at first terrified, then embarrassed—were angry at everyone.

We realize teachers have more than enough to do. Yet as people in a unique position to make an enormous difference in the lives of children, they have some distinct responsibilities. They have a responsibility:

- ❖ to take a strong stand for the child's best interest;
- ❖ to encourage both parents to participate in school conferences;
- ❖ to make sure both households receive important papers and notices;
- ❖ to encourage parents to work with each other for the benefit of their children.

Can you really expect all this of your child's teacher? Yes, you can. "I know all about the pressures teachers face," Nancy says. "I used to teach handicapped children in the public schools. I had to fill out federal, state, and local forms on a daily basis, so I know the time constraints. But I also know that teachers who make the effort will ultimately help the child perform better in class, and the child's behavior problems will decrease. So I would say this to teachers who are loath to get involved: 'You will be doing it for the child, but in the end, you will also be doing it for yourself.'"

To parents we would say: *Give the school a break.* There is only so much they can do. They are worried about liability and they have to protect themselves. If you pour out your conflicts with your ex to your child's teacher, that teacher is going to have to walk a tightrope between parents. She may not be able to give your child what he needs because she is so afraid of upsetting either you or your ex—or one of your attorneys.

"Then what *should* I do?" you may be asking.

If at all possible, go with your ex to the school and say, "We may no longer be together as a family, but we still work together for our children. We both care about them and want to do what is best for them. Please call both of us for conferences. We will do our best to relay school information to each other, but it would help us a great deal to have you send duplicate notices for things such as assignments, field trips, and so forth." You may want to supply them with self-addressed, stamped envelopes. This lets the school off the hook. And you both will be more likely to get the information you need.

MORE POWER TO YOU!

Grandparents, aunts, uncles, cousins, family friends — they all have a great deal to add to your blended family. Each of you should be able to have pleasant, free interactions with them. Each of you should be able to love these important people without incurring the anger of someone else. None of you should have to endure the stress of turmoil stirred up by extended family. That's what *should* be.

If that's not how it is, talk to your family and friends. Let them know that your children's identity depends on their feelings about the families to which they belong. Assure those extended family members that they have an important role to play in your family, one that can never be filled as well by any other person.

Treasure the involvement of others in the life of your blended family. Encourage and support your ex-in-laws' desire to share in your child's joyous occasions. Respect the basic nature, temperament, and interests of your child and how they fit with the temperament and interests of each individual relative.

How much richer your family will be!

Chapter 6

BROTHERS AND SISTERS

*Prepare for Wild
and Wonderful Combinations*

For almost a month, Lauren's third-grade class had been working on their family histories. One entire wall of the classroom was decorated with a world map surrounded by the names of the children, with arrows pointing to the countries of their ancestry. Lauren's arrows pointed to Sweden, Ireland, and Italy. For the international family night dinner, she brought spaghetti with Swedish meatballs. On display were the autobiographies the children had written.

Back at home, Lauren showed her autobiography to Angela, her stepmother. *My mommy is Barbara and my daddy is Howard,* Lauren had written. *My other mother is Angela and my other father is Brian. I have nine brothers and sisters.*

Angela stopped reading and looked at Lauren in confusion. "Nine brothers and sisters? You don't have nine. There are two brothers and one sister at your mother's house and two sisters here. That's five."

"You forgot the others," Lauren said. "Ross has two boys and one girl, and Cassie has a baby boy. That makes nine."

Lauren was right. Angela had forgotten that her stepdaughter's mother had been in two other marriages—Ross was the other husband—and that her own husband had been married another time to Cassie. Although Cassie and Brian had no children, Cassie had just remarried and given birth to her first child.

When you start talking about all the variables, don't forget the child's point of view. You may find that the picture gets quite complex.

"Lauren's autobiography was wonderful," Angela told us later. "The most poignant thing was the way she used pronouns so accurately and so matter-of-factly—ours, mine, hers, his. She made the whole crazy family thing seem natural; it made so much sense to her. And all those nine children, even the ones I knew nothing about, were important parts of her life. They were her brothers and sisters."

YOUR CHILD'S EXTENDED FAMILY

"When I saw how Lauren felt about those children I hardly knew existed, I decided to make some changes," Angela said. "I decided to look at everyone from a different perspective; not a legal one—legally, Lauren had no bond to some of those kids—but through Lauren's emotional eyes."

On Lauren's birthday, Angela invited all the girl's brothers and sisters to her party. She also put their birthdays on the family calendar so she could remind Lauren to send cards to them.

"It really didn't take that much effort, yet it meant so much to Lauren," Angela said.

Angela is a wise parent. As blended family parents, we are constantly either putting pieces together in the family puzzle, or we are confusing the picture by taking pieces out.

EXTENDED BY ASSOCIATION

Several years ago, our family was at a football game, watching Brent play. Brent's three-year-old half-brother Gregory was there, too. Although Gregory is no relation to Joanna and Carley, the girls see him so often they feel he's part of their extended family.

All afternoon the girls took turns playing with Gregory. Late in the day, Carley ran over to Laura, Gregory's mother, and said, "Could you watch Gregory a minute for me? I have to go to the bathroom." Carley saw Gregory as her responsibility.

"He's sort of like a half-half-brother," Carley says of the boy, "because he's my half-brother's half-brother."

If you were to ask a child to draw a picture of the people most important to him, that picture would likely include family members, friends, perhaps a neighbor or a teacher—and maybe the half-sibling of a brother or sister. That shouldn't be surprising. Even though there may be no relationship between the children, they may see themselves as part of an extended family. They both come to special events, they are both present at important family outings, and most important, they have a family member in common.

"My four-year-old Samantha was born to my husband and me, but in her mind she has 'another dad,'" Marianne said. "The thing is, her two older sisters—my daughters from my first marriage—go to visit their other dad every week. Samantha figured, 'If my sisters have another dad, then I must, too.'"

Marianne, deciding she should clear up the matter with her daughter, sat Samantha down and explained the situation as best she could. When she finished, she said, "So you see, Samantha, your sisters have another father, but you don't. Daddy is your only father."

Samantha thought for a minute. "Well, then," she said, "can I go with them to visit *their* other dad?"

Her sisters thought that was a great idea. They asked

their dad, then they asked Marianne and Peter. And, sure enough, Samantha sometimes goes along on "bisitation." While she's there, she calls him Dad just like her sisters do.

"In her mind Samantha knows that man is not her father," Marianne says. "But in her heart, she has 'another dad.'"

BEYOND THE LEGAL

"But he is not really your brother," one mother explained to her child who couldn't understand why his stepfather's son couldn't live with them. "Legally, you aren't related at all. You might be good friends, but you are not brothers."

While that mother is right, her legal definition meant nothing to her son. Kids aren't impressed by such things. But the boy surely couldn't miss the message his mom was sending: *In no way is he your brother.*

Marianne allows her child to go on "bisitation." Angela makes a point of including her stepdaughter's other blended sisters and brothers. We accept our children's relationship with Gregory. Who is important in your child's life? What are you doing to show acceptance of and respect for those special relationships?

A REARRANGED PECKING ORDER

Chad loved being an only child. When he was with his mother, she smothered him with attention. When he was with his father and his stepmother, they spoiled him. Then his mom got remarried. Along with a stepfather, he got a stepbrother, Alex, who was five years older than Chad.

"I like Alex all right," Chad said. "He helps me with my homework and shoots baskets with me in the driveway. But other times he calls me a little brat and makes me stay out of his room and won't let me touch his stuff. I liked it better when I was the only kid."

Just as Chad was beginning to adjust to being the little kid of the family, his mom announced she was expecting another child. Baby Hannah was born two weeks after Chad's eighth birthday.

"She's their favorite," Chad sulked. "Everyone says she is so cute. Everything she does is so exciting. When I ask mom to do something with me, she says, 'Oh, I have to feed Hannah now.' Dad always yells at me to pick up my stuff so the baby won't get into it. Everyone likes her best."

Who can blame poor Chad for being confused and frustrated? Within the space of a couple years he has had to go from the pampered position of only child, the center of his parents' life, to being stuck into the unenviable spot of middle child, bossed around by his older brother and outperformed by a baby sister. Chad explained his position in two words: "Left out."

Rick and his son Darren had always been close. When Rick remarried, Darren got a stepbrother, and he wasn't at all happy about it. Yet as time went on, the boys grew closer and closer. They played ball together, they bought an old clunker car and worked on it together, they even double-dated.

Then came the news: Their parents were divorcing. Darren was crushed. "How can you do this to me, Dad?" he asked.

"Don't feel so bad, Son," Rick said. "It will be like it used to be, just you and me."

But it could never really be that way again. Their blended family had become a strong unit. Darren and his stepbrother were best friends.

"Just move on with your life," Rick said.

"I can't," Darren told him.

Throughout the pain and anger of the divorce, Darren and his ex-brother stayed in contact. But it was never the same. They were no longer a family.

KIDS CAN'T BE COMPARED

"Janie is the good one of the bunch. We never have any trouble with her."

"Freddie is the musical one. His brother wants to take trumpet lessons like Freddie does, but his brother doesn't have talent. It isn't worth investing money in him."

"John is the smart one. If just one of our kids can go to college, it should be him."

"Susie is the pretty one. We don't rush her in the morning, even if it means everyone else has to wait to get into the bathroom. Her looks are what's going to get her through life."

Many families cannot understand how damaging it is to compare kids with one another and label them. Some do it in a negative way ("Henry is a computer nerd. No wonder he doesn't have any friends. Steven has friends all right. What he doesn't have is brains"). Others think they are being positive ("Mary is the prettiest girl in this family. She'll never have trouble finding a man. But don't you worry, Kim. With your brains, you don't need looks"). Either way, by comparing you are pointing up areas for competition and jealousy, and you are making judgments on what you think is valuable and worthwhile.

Sure, Henry is different from Steven, and Mary is different than Kim. That's how God created us: each different and unique. And aren't you glad? Wouldn't the world be boring if everyone in it was just like you? It sure would be a disaster if everyone was like either of us! Instead of pitting your kids against each other, celebrate their differences.

"That sounds fine," you may be saying, "but in my family, one child really is a lot smarter than the other (or more athletic, or a better musician, or better looking). How can I be positive about that?"

By changing your attitude. If you think the difference is a negative, then look at it as a challenge rather than as something to ruin the child's life. Many brilliant people have failed to accomplish much in life, while people with much lower IQs have been fantastically successful. Klutzy people, people who cannot carry a tune, and downright ugly people can lead wonderfully fulfilling and worthwhile lives. It happens every day.

When you are tempted to compare you children, congratulate them instead:

"All right, Henry! You can do wonders on that computer."

"Steve, with you around, the house is always filled with laughter and fun."

"Mary, you got a B on that history paper. Good going!"

"Kim, you look lovely in that new dress you made. Wait a minute, let me get my camera!"

As you put value in differences, and as you nurture and build them up, watch your children blossom and grow. As they get older and move into adulthood, you will be amazed at the exciting twists and turns those wonderful differences will take.

FAMILIES GROW AND CHANGE

When we married, our family was just us and our two six-year-old boys. That's how we started out. But our family didn't stay there for long. In the ten years we have been a family, we have grown in three specific ways: Carley, Joanna, and Michelle. Each child entered our family in a different and special way.

BIRTH CHILDREN

Carley was born to us. From the beginning, we knew we wanted a child together. The boys were seven when we learned Nancy was pregnant. We wanted them to appreciate the pregnancy, and we also thought it would be an excellent and natural opportunity for sex education. So we talked to our ex-spouses about our talking openly and frankly with the boys. It was a positive experience for all of us, and it helped make the boys a part of the new baby's arrival.

In blended families, new babies can be a worrisome matter for kids already in the family. This new child won't have one parent and one stepparent in the house like the other kids do. From the beginning, this baby will be the child of both mother and father. The kids will invariably wonder: *Will Mom and Dad love this baby more than they love me?* Don't wait for the problem to come up. Let your children know about the new addition to your family from the early stages of pregnancy. Continually assure them of your love. In your words, deeds, and attitudes, tell them: "Every one of our children is equally precious to us."

ADOPTED CHILDREN
Joanna entered our family by adoption.

Our law practices were going great. We were both bringing in nice fat salaries, and bonuses besides. And we had three great kids. Our home and our lives were full to the brim—not to mention a little crazy.

A favorite part of Nancy's practice was handling adoptions. So when a television program ran a piece on the plight of abandoned Romanian children existing in asylums and institutions in that country, Nancy's phone began to ring. "Did you see the program?" everyone wanted to know. Nancy had not.

But then a strange thing happened. A few weeks before Christmas of 1990, Nancy had an overwhelming conviction that a little Romanian girl was to live with us. "It was scary," Nancy recalls. "Another child was the last thing I needed! The idea was absolutely ridiculous. It made no sense at all. My usual response to anything that popped into my mind was to blurt it out to Bill, but this seemed too foolish to mention even to him. So I kept my mouth shut."

After a week, still unable to shake the idea, Nancy did broach the subject to Bill. His response astounded her: "I've had the exact same thought! But it was so bizarre, I couldn't bring myself to mention it to you."

We became so convinced this was something we were supposed to do that we didn't really worry about how it was going to come about. Nancy called people she had done agency work for to inquire about how to proceed in a foreign adoption. Our good friend Dr. Lorraine Boisselle of the Adoption Centre said, "Nancy, I have been to Romania and it is a mess. I really think you should forget this."

On Christmas Eve, Lorraine called and told us about an American newborn baby who needed minor surgery on her ear. "If you want to adopt a little girl who needs you, I'll place this baby with you," she offered.

We said we would pray about it.

"The picture that won't leave my mind isn't a baby in this country," Nancy told Bill. "It's a little girl in Romania."

We thanked our friend for her help but told her no. Then we added, "But, please, go through your files again. There must be an adoptable little girl in Romania."

She did, and there was. "The child is four years old and has been abandoned," Lorraine told us. Then she quickly added, "But you should know she has health problems. Are you *sure* this is what you want?"

There was no question in our minds.

Lorraine sent a fax to the Intercontinental Hotel in Bucharest, one of the only fax machines in Romania at the time. The reply came back stating that if we were interested, one of us would have to come to Romania. The child had a living birth mother, it turned out, and she wouldn't sign a consent form until she met one of us.

Lorraine handed us a picture. "Here she is," she said. The picture showed three little girls. One was darling, with a bright vivacious face.

"She's beautiful!" Nancy cried.

"No," Lorraine said. She pointed to the solemn,

expressionless child next to her. "This is the one. This is Joanna."

It only took one day to say, "Yes, we want her." Whatever the problems, whatever the hurdles, we knew she was our child.

Nancy was all set to pack her bags for Romania, but Bill wasn't so sure. It was during the time of the Persian Gulf war, and President Bush had warned Americans not to fly into Frankfurt and London, let alone into East Europe.

"Put the trip off for a while," Bill said. "You can go when things calm down."

"A strange thing happened to me," Nancy says. "Usually I try to butt in on everything, especially when I feel strongly about an issue, but this time I stayed really calm. I prayed, *Okay God, it's up to you. If you want me to go, you'll have to change Bill's heart.*"

A few days later, Nancy underwent a minor surgical procedure. When she woke up, Bill said, "I spent the whole day making arrangements for your trip to Romania." Her prayer had been answered.

Five days later, Nancy arrived in Romania, armed with impressive letters from the governor of Florida, and references from Florida Supreme Court Justice Ben Overton who had helped the Romanians write their constitution. Romania in February was bitterly cold and depressingly dreary. There was limited electricity, and public buildings were choked with cigarette smoke. But Nancy did meet Joanna, and she fell in love immediately.

Nancy returned home carrying videos of little Joanna, and for the first time, we started to worry. We were adopting a child! We had already fallen in love with her. What if something happened and she never got here?

Our worries were for naught. Joanna arrived the night before Mother's Day. Two weeks later, Romanian adoptions were closed to the world.

Joanna did not appear to be the ideal sister for our

children. She spoke no English, and all we had was a list of 100 Romanian words. The abuse and neglect the little girl had suffered had taken their toll: Joanna hit and bit herself, and she screamed and spit at us. And we had been told she was borderline mentally retarded, so we had that "low intelligence" label hanging in the back of our minds. But once again, we were in for a surprise. Not only is Joanna physically and mentally healthy, she is a mentally gifted child! God's grace, good counseling, patience, and Nancy's educational experience all helped.

We don't want to give the idea that expanding a family by adoption is easy, nor that it is for everyone. It certainly isn't. Nancy always warns her adoptive parents against setting their expectations too high. Like every other parenting situation, adoption comes with no guarantee of a happy ending.

Michelle's entry into our family was truly unique. Last year, Joanna's birth mother in Romania contacted us. "Please adopt my older daughter, too," she begged. "Give her a better chance at life than I can give her here." The girl was fifteen years old, knew limited English, and had no experience in the kind of life we lead in this society. We saw this situation as having the potential to really upset the family balance we had worked so hard to achieve. On the other hand, this might be Michelle's only chance at a decent life. And she was Joanna's sister. How could we refuse?

Michelle's entry into the family required a great deal of adjusting on everyone's part. Joanna and Carley could no longer have their own rooms. Neither could Michelle, who was used to being an only child and having her own space. Our family rules didn't go over well with Michelle, yet we couldn't have a whole separate set of rules for her than for the other kids.

We anticipated many of the transitional changes, but some were totally unexpected. From Joanna's birth until she was sent to the hospital at the age of two, her big sister Michelle had been a primary caretaker. "Michelle is my mommy," Joanna stated the day Michelle arrived. But Michelle had no interest in being anyone's mommy. It was a tough couple of weeks, but in time, Joanna came back to being our little girl and looking to Nancy as her mother.

Michelle and our boys get along well. Sometimes they go out as a group with their friends. It was Brent who helped her study for her driver's test, and he even took her to get her license.

ALL IN THE FAMILY

Brothers and sisters. However they enter the family, and regardless of your relationship to each of your children's siblings, they are all a vital part of your kids' lives.

When your puzzle is not fitting together the way you think it should, when the kids fight and argue and yell that they hate each other, when you see alliances between certain kids while others are left outside to fend for themselves, remember: People can and do change. Don't look at family relationships as a snapshot and assume that it is the way everyone is always going to be. Kids grow and change. Many a brother and sister in an intact family fought like cats and dogs growing up, only to be best friends as adults. Blended families are no different.

Time can be a great healer. Nick remembers that when Joanna first came she spit at him and threw things and destroyed things in the house. That's not easy for an adolescent to watch. And yet, in recent months, the two of them have really tightened their relationship. Joanna always points out how her skin is brown like Nick's or her smile is big like Mom's. She loves those physical connections she can see and touch. They are important to her because they make her feel she belongs. Things do change.

When you find yourself saying, "But two weeks ago they had this really awful fight . . .," stop in mid-sentence and ask yourself, "Is it any better today?"

"Michelle and I spend a lot of time together," Carley told a friend recently. "I can talk to her and she understands about problems in school. We understand each other, and we have nicknames for each other. The more I know her, the nicer she is."

Carley and Michelle are sisters.

Chapter 7

MONEY
MADNESS

Where to Put Your Focus

For stepbrothers Joel and Blake, it was a great day. Their soccer team had made it to the playoffs. All their moms were there to cheer them on, Joel's mom Ellie, Blake's stepmom Anne, and Blake's mom Karen.

"Anne was chattering on about her tennis and golf lessons, and Ellie chimed in about her tennis team," Karen recalls. "And then there was me. Pregnant and working until the last minute because I couldn't afford to quit, I was frantically trying to do my paperwork and still watch the game. As I listened to all the golf and tennis talk, my resentment grew. All I could think was: *I'm doing all this work just to be able to support these women!*"

Of all the elements of family blending, Karen has the most adamant feelings about the money: "I get so angry!" she says. Perhaps you can relate.

When it comes to money concerns, we know how easy it is to become resentful. We really do. We've been there. But we also know how counterproductive resentment is.

"I don't care," you may be saying. "I pay child support and that money goes right into the pocket of my ex-spouse. Why should I have to pay my ex?"

We would say, you have a problem—a focus problem.

FOCUS ON YOUR CHILD

Sacrifices come along with divorce. That's the way it is. But we want to go on record as saying: *As much as possible your children should not be the ones having to make those sacrifices.* In theory, most people agree with this principle. But then the almighty dollar takes over and blurs the issue.

We have found that a request for primary custody, or for more time with the child, can sometimes be a cover for a parent's hidden agenda—a way to minimize the amount of money one parent will have to pay out to the other. Mediators see these hidden agendas. So do judges and attorneys. And in time, they will become apparent to the children as well.

Children who don't receive support from their parents are well aware of it, and you can be sure they are affected by it. Shaquille O'Neal, Orlando Magic All-Star, is a good example. His biological father, Joe Toney, who had abandoned Shaq and his mother when Shaq was tiny, suddenly wants to get to know his now-famous son. Shaquille wants nothing to do with the man. Here's how he explained it to a reporter from the *Orlando Sentinel:* "Just because you bring a child into the world, it doesn't make you a father. . . . He wasn't around the first 21 years, and he won't be around the next 21. . . ."

When it comes to their kids, parents can be amazingly stingy. Very few of the children of divorce in Judith Wallerstein's study received financial help with their college expenses, even though most of their fathers were themselves college graduates. To make matters worse, many young people found themselves blocked from receiving financial aid because their fathers' incomes were too high. Fewer than half the young people surveyed were attending or had completed college as opposed to an expected average of 85 percent. When fathers did help their children with college costs, they were twice as likely to help their sons as their daughters.

"But my having to pay all that support money is unfair! Every time I write that check, my blood boils!"

We know. But think of it this way: When you write that check, you are not writing it for your ex-spouse. You are writing it for your child. Train yourself to make this your focus. You say that will be mighty hard to do? Yes it will, but do it anyway. If you don't, it will pain you every time you write the check, and every month it will hurt more.

Sometimes your resolve will be pushed to the limit. Maureen's husband received this letter from his ex-wife:

Dear Rob,

I would like you to continue paying support for our son until he is twenty-two years old. I think it would be best if he stayed at home and lived with me while he attends college.

Sincerely,
Louise

Furious, Maureen wrote a letter of her own:

Dear ex-wife of my husband and mother of my stepson,

This is a letter that will never be sent, not for your sake but because it would cause too much friction between my stepson's two families. But I am dying to let you know how I feel. For years my husband has been paying very good support for his son, only to see him again and again dressed in rags and outgrown clothes. You, on the other hand, were always outfitted in the best tennis wear money could buy. And you always managed to afford your country club and tennis tournaments, and your trips all over the country. Your travel and fun and expensive clothes cost my stepson his future.

Our legal obligation for your son ends on his eighteenth birthday, which is in February of his senior year in high school. Considering how much time he spends at our house, it would probably be fair for us not to send the payments through his June high school graduation. However, we know you depend on that money since you have never worked more than part-time since the divorce over twelve years ago.

We have already talked to you, and then to a counselor, of our concerns about a number of your parenting practices. The counselor also was concerned, but you didn't hear that because you chose not to participate in the counseling sessions. Suffice it to say that it clearly would not be in the boy's best interest for him to live at home with you throughout his college years.

Please, please, for the sake of my stepson, get a life of your own and let the boy go.

Most Sincerely,
Your son's angry stepmother

No, Maureen did not send the letter. But she did show it to her husband, and together they made a decision based not on money but on the boy's best interests: Rob did not continue to pay support, but he agreed to send the same amount of money to his son monthly as long as he attended college—away from his mother's house.

When you focus on the children, you may find that money matters will take a twist or a turn. What do you do when one child has special needs? What if those needs are financially exorbitant? What if they adversely affect the rest of the family? What should your commitment be, and to whom, and for how much?

HONOR YOUR COMMITMENTS

Your commitments should be to your obligations. And if the obligation is your spouse's? Then, stepparent, it is yours as well.

"Why is so much of your salary going to support them?" Valerie demanded of her husband Jeff. "Your ex-wife is remarried and her new husband makes lots of money. He can take care of those kids much more easily than you can. So why are you still on the hook?"

This reasoning makes perfect sense to Valerie. But in the context of child support, it makes no sense at all. No, Valerie, *the birth parents are responsible for their children, regardless of who else comes along.*

"The problem is that my husband pays way too much," Valerie insisted. "He always has. Whenever his ex-wife said she needed more money, he added a bit to the check. Now he is really overpaying, and we cannot afford it."

Certain things that happen in the divorce or settlement, or in the ongoing divorce relationship, are functions of the personalities involved. Everything goes along all right, but then a new spouse enters who is a different kind of person. Suddenly the parenting relationship is thrown off. Jeff's motto always was: *Don't sweat the small stuff.* He was supposed to pay $400 a month, but it had worked its way up to $500 a month. The extra amount was no big deal to Jeff. He figured the kids needed it.

Unlike Jeff, Valerie was a detail person. When she saw that Jeff was paying an extra $100 a month, she said, "It isn't right! It isn't fair! Quit paying that extra money. If she insists on it, take her to court and fight it."

To some extent, a new spouse needs to look at the established pattern and adapt to it. If we were to ask

Valerie what she loves about Jeff, she would likely say, "I love his whole being. I love his personality, his demeanor, and his entire outlook on life." The fact is, Jeff's easy-going approach to life is part of why Valerie loves him.

A new spouse who enters the picture and then tries to change it is asking for trouble. Certainly the new spouse can discuss her feelings with the parent. It may be that he will agree with her. But if not, in most cases the new spouse should defer to the parent.

Valerie would not defer. "It's a matter of principle!" she insisted. And so she pestered and nagged and complained and condemned until Jeff threw his hands in the air and said, "Okay, you win! I'll do it your way!" The next month Jeff's ex-wife received a check for $400 and a terse note stating that the overpayments would stop immediately. Furious, she told the children in no uncertain terms what she thought about their cheap, uncaring father and the witch he was married to. The winners in that case? We don't see any. But we certainly see the losers.

Making changes in some of your external commitments might make it easier for all of you. For instance, in most cases it's better not to continue to own a house together with your ex-spouse. It will be an ongoing area for argument ("Does the house really need a new roof?" "Why did you hire a plumber? You know how overpriced they are! I could have fixed the leak myself!" "Just because you want to sell the house in three years doesn't mean I want to!" "What do you mean your cousin is going to be the realtor? I don't think so!"). If you have to retain joint ownership, keep disputes to a minimum by laying out all the specifics about when things will take place ("We will put a new roof on the house one year from this summer"), how you will deal with repairs ("We will get three quotes and decide together which to go with"), how the payment will be made ("He will pay 60 percent and she will pay 40 percent"), and so forth.

As much as possible, trim away areas that will foster

conflict and encourage manipulation.

HANDLING MANIPULATION

Madelyn knew she should feel fortunate; her ex-husband Randy never complained about paying child support. In fact, he was generous. Very generous. *Overly* generous. When the girls were with him, he would drop them off at the mall with his credit card. When his son was there, the two of them would spend hours in the computer store, and they never left empty-handed.

"I *love* going to Dad's!" the kids would exclaim.

"No wonder," Madelyn would mumble. "It's always Christmas over there."

When Madelyn complained to Randy, he shrugged it off with, "Hey, I like to do it. After all they've been through, they deserve to be spoiled a little. I can afford it, so what's the big deal?"

"The big deal is, they don't need all that stuff!" Madelyn shot back. "Those girls can't live long enough to wear all the clothes they have. They wear something once or twice, then they give it to a girlfriend. And Jay has so much computer stuff he can't even put it all away. It's piled everywhere."

"It makes them happy," Randy said. "That's all that matters to me."

This tug on the children may be an outright manipulation of them ("If I buy them what they want, they will love me best") or it may be a more subtle manipulation of values ("Okay, you go right ahead and stress the value of intangibles. I'll demonstrate the value of a well-placed dollar!"). Regardless of how much money you have or don't have, there always seems to be a tension when children are going between two households: Where should the money be spent? Where are the priorities? How much is too much? When is it time to say no?

We know one family in which an eight-year-old girl announced to her father, "Mommy is buying me a horse, and she's getting me riding lessons!" Not only did her father know nothing about this, he was the one expected to pay the bills.

"I can afford it," he told us, "but I don't happen to think an eight-year-old should own a horse. That money could be spent in a much better way. I mean, why not get her the riding lessons first and see if it's something she will stick with and love?"

The child got the horse. In the end her father figured, "If I tell her no when she is so excited about it, I'll be the bad guy yet again." His manipulative ex-wife knew exactly what she was doing.

A manipulative father told his sixteen-year-old son, "Come live with me and I'll buy you a motorcycle and a car. Then Mom will have to pay child support to me."

This manipulation of the kids can come back to haunt parents. Counselor Fran Holt told us, "One thing I see a lot in my work is young people who have grown up feeling extremely guilty for having gone to live with their other parent just so they could get the gifts. We are having to do a lot of repair work on these kids when they get older. When kids mature and realize what was done, they often flip-flop and turn their anger on the parent who took advantage of them by buying their affection and loyalty with a bribe."

Of course, parents are not the only ones who stoop to manipulation. Kids can be masters of the art. This is true in intact families as well, but the problem is exacerbated in blended families. And the kids can begin the process at a surprisingly young age. ("If you won't buy me the dolly, I'll ask Mommy. She will because she loves me!") Wise parents and stepparents will be on their guard and will not allow themselves to fall into the manipulation trap.

Meg and Tony's four blended-family kids were so manipulative that Meg had come to dread Christmas. "No matter how I planned or what I got for the kids, it was never enough," she said. "I was at my wit's end.

Then I hit upon a plan that really worked for us."

Together Meg and Tony laid out a budget for Christmas spending, allotting the same amount for each child. Then they made plans for Tony's annual Christmas bonus, which was always substantial. "Since his success in business was actually the success of the entire family, we decided to percentage it out," Meg said. "Family needs were taken off the top. Then Tony got 30 percent of what was left, I got 20 percent, and we divided up the other 50 percent between the kids. Not only did the kids love being able to use their bonus money any way they chose, it made it seem more like we were all in this together.

"One year we had to put a new roof on the house. After that was paid for, there wasn't much bonus money left to divvy up. But not a single child complained. One said philosophically, 'Even if we only get to go to a movie and get tubs of popcorn and giant sodas, it's still *our* bonus, and it's still fun spending it.'"

GIVE AND TAKE, BACK AND FORTH

A recent article in the *Orlando Sentinel* stated: "The average married couple spends four minutes a day in meaningful conversation."

Just think. With shared parenting, if you're not careful, you might end up spending more time talking to your ex-spouse than to your current spouse! Sad, isn't it? Perhaps noncommunication is why so many couples have trouble understanding where the support money is going, why the parent holds on to that monetary obligation, and why the stepparent is balking at the payments.

Nancy has done many radio talk shows on the subject of child support. Again and again stepmothers call in and say, "I just don't know why we should have to write that check to his ex-wife." One even said, "My husband writes the check every month, and every month I tear it up. I'm not about to send her that money. Why should I?

We need it right here in our own family!"

Unless those couples do some pretty intensive talking and listening, they are headed for big trouble.

Let's think again about that the-money-isn't-really-going-for-the-kids objection. If that has been hanging you up, we suggest you confront it straight on. You might say, "I've noticed that when Junior comes over, his jeans have holes and his shirts are outgrown. Is there a problem we need to discuss?" If your ex-spouse says, "Yes, you can give me more money," you might say, "I'm sorry, that's not a possibility. But I would be happy to take some of the money I already send and go look at consignment shops or thrift stores and see if we can't get more for that money." That way you can concentrate your concern on your child.

On the other hand, your ex may respond with something like, "The money you send simply won't stretch that far. Clothing and food are just a small part of the cost of raising a child. I don't think you know how much I do spend on him." She may have a valid point. Here again communication can prove to be the solution.

It costs a lot to raise a child, and many of the costs are not as apparent as new jeans and T-shirts and sneakers. For instance, mom would be able to get along with a one-bedroom apartment if she were alone, but since she's raising a child, she needs a two-bedroom apartment, which costs more. Her transportation needs are different and her gasoline costs are higher. So are her utilities and telephone bill. She pays more for health insurance, buys more bandages and cough syrup and children's aspirin. She buys cookies for school parties and orange juice for the soccer team and bags of chips for after-school snacks. She pays for movie tickets, admission to the zoo, and club membership dues.

If you are not the primary parent, you might not see the request for the three dozen cupcakes for the school bake sale, or the field trip slip telling you to return it with $7.50, or the price for the uniform required for the soccer team.

If you and your ex are battling over how the support money is spent, consider mediation. You will each have the opportunity to stand in the other's shoes and see how they fit.

"In my capacity as mediator, I sometimes ask a father to write out a budget for the mother," Nancy says. "The mother starts by providing him with a financial statement listing all the things she has to consider in raising the child, from the price of shoes to the cost of vitamins. Then I give the list to the dad and say, 'Here's what she has. Now you come up with a priorities list for her and a budget.'"

Then Nancy has the two come back in a week. Almost always the father says to his ex-wife, "You know, I've decided the child support I'm paying is fine. We don't have to talk about it any more."

Education and communication are the keys. It's important to get together and talk about budgets. Some people can do it on their own, but many need a mediator, a neutral party specifically trained to help facilitate communication between and options for these families.

"What if my income changes?" you may ask. "What if I've lost my high-paying job and am now earning far less money?"

Another may say, "But my ex-wife was in school full time when the support was set. Now she earns as much as I do. Doesn't she have an equal obligation?"

Good questions. Again we would say, talk with a mediator. This is a good idea any time you need to modify your support order. You say a mediator costs too much? Not in the long run. Don't think of it as an expense. Think of it as an investment in your child.

INSURANCE CONCERNS

What do you know about your ex-spouse's health insurance? How about life insurance coverage? Have you talked about wills?

"Hey," you may say, "I can understand talking about

child support and discipline problems. But *insurance?* Why?"

Because it affects your child, that's why. And it may well affect your new family, too.

"We talked about it right after the divorce. What is going to change?"

In many cases, plenty. In today's economy, companies are doing everything they can to save money. They make changes in policies, up the deductible, and add in more exceptions. Those changes can affect all of you.

HEALTH INSURANCE

Until he was eleven, Philip was a healthy, active, average-sized boy. Then he suddenly stopped growing. All his friends shot up past him. "You'll get a growth spurt soon," his mother Eve assured him. But he didn't. So Eve started taking her son from doctor to doctor. Finally, when Philip was sixteen and still 4 foot 10, he got the news he had been praying for: There was a hormone he could take that would solve his problem. But his joy was short-lived. The treatment would cost $4,000 a month, and it would have to be continued for up to four years!

"It's experimental, so my insurance won't cover it," Philip's father explained. "I'm really sorry, but there's no way I can possibly pay $200,000."

Philip got the growth hormone, and he is now a normal 5 foot 8 inches tall. How did it happen? Eve's husband's insurance covered it.

Even though you will probably never find yourself in such a drastic situation, Philip's story emphasizes the need to coordinate everyone's policies. Read them through and determine

❖ which one can offer your child the best coverage;
❖ which one will allow you to choose the best doctor for the child;

❖ which doctors are covered, if you choose an
   HMO, and will these doctors meet your child's
   needs;
❖ which policy has the most reasonable rates;
❖ which one has the deduction option you prefer.

When you agree upon an insurance plan, the parent
on that plan should immediately get an insurance card for
the other parent. That way either parent can take the child
in for treatment. Now there is even a legal way to reim-
burse the nonemployee parent via a federal statute. Ask
the person who does the billing for your health care
provider about it.

LIFE INSURANCE

Both you and your ex-spouse should have life insurance
so that if one of you should die, the other could keep the
kids without having to make disastrous changes in their
lifestyle.

Most people get a minimum amount of life insurance
through their employer. If you are quite young, you can
get it for very little money. If you are older, it may be too
costly, especially if you have a pre-existing medical con-
dition. But do what you have to in order to provide some
financial protection for your children.

Some parents have their children purchase a life
insurance policy on the parent's life, and then provide
the money for the premiums. If your children cannot be
depended upon to keep the premiums paid, a life insurance trust may be a better choice.

An insurance policy also allows parents who don't
have big estates to give their children an immediate
inheritance. The new spouse can inherit the estate, including the house and bank account, and the children would
inherit the money from the insurance policy.

Whatever your arrangements, be sure to talk them
over with your present (or better yet, soon-to-be) spouse:

"I have $200,000 in life insurance. I've contracted $150,000 of that for the security of my children in the event of my death. That means $50,000 will be left for you. Is that enough, or do you think we should get more?" Be sure your spouse understands that your commitment to your children is not going to change.

Wills

If you are divorced, have you made out a new will? Has your new spouse made a will? It's important to do so, because upon your divorce, your old will became outdated. In any case, should you die, your children will be raised by their other parent. That happens automatically in almost every state.

"Wait!" you may say. "What if the stepparent was the one who had been raising the child?"

It makes no difference. Unless the parent is incapable of caring for the child, that's where the child will go. If there is a serious problem—substance abuse, mental incompetence, or abuse of the child, for instance—consult an attorney immediately. You may want to address specific custody instructions.

PLAN FOR SUCCESS

Good marriages are built on good communication, and in blended families, there is more that needs to be communicated. Sit down with your future spouse immediately and go over this checklist:

- ❖ Tell each other what you own and what you owe.
- ❖ Discuss your financial goals in life.
- ❖ Review your wills, and rewrite them if necessary. Determine what you want to leave to each other, what you want to leave to your children together, and what you want to leave to your children from your previous marriages.

✤ Review your life insurance. Determine the best way to provide for your children should something happen to you. Also consider what each of you will need in the absence of the other.

✤ Look into the advisability of changing the beneficiaries on both your life insurance and retirement plans.

GIFTS OF TIME

"I'm depressed," you might be saying. "My finances are so tight that I have little money to manage. I feel bad that I can't be more generous with my children."

Let us leave you with this assurance: Money isn't everything.

"I remember when I was a single parent, just Brent and me," Nancy says. "I had no money, I mean *none!* But I sure did have time. When Brent was with his dad, I would clean our tiny 450-square foot house, and then it was just me alone, waiting for Brent to come home. Brent's dad could buy him so much more than I could, but I decided I could give my son the gift of my time. I painted his furniture and fixed up his room especially for him. Those years taught me a lesson I've never forgotten: Gifts of time can mean more than the gifts money can buy."

Do your best to manage your money wisely, but don't waste time or energy lamenting your lean budget. Instead, ask yourself what you can do that will be special and meaningful to the kids.

A few years ago we decided it was time to redo Nick and Brent's bedroom the way they wanted it done. They wanted futons instead of beds, and they decided they wanted the room painted black. We said okay to the futons, but nixed the black walls. We did, however, agree to their second choice—splatter painting the room. Nancy will probably have purple paint on some part of her body for the rest of her life!

What special things can you do for your kids? Shoot

baskets on the driveway in the evening with them despite weariness? Fix the macaroni and cheese she so loves for dinner? Take the time—and the patience—to teach your newly "of age" young person to drive? Be willing to help out at school when everyone else is too busy? Volunteer to drive for the field trip? Teach the child to play chess?

The best thing you can give your child is yourself, and it will cost you nothing.

Chapter 8

GLIDING OUT THE GLITCHES

*How to Handle All the Changes
with Some Grace*

C harlotte knows a lot about blended families. She
has been married twice and is twice divorced.

After her first divorce, Charlotte agreed that her
two sons, ages eight and ten, should continue to live with
Ken, their dad, in the family home. Charlotte moved
three hundred miles away to be near her parents in Iowa.

"I had no money and no way of supporting myself,"
Charlotte said. "Our kids had lived in the same house their
entire lives, they had always gone to the same school, and
all their friends were there. It made absolutely no sense to
move them away from Missouri." No one paid child support, and Charlotte and Ken shared custody. "I had the
boys all summer, at Christmas, and during spring break.
Every other Friday night, Ken and I met at a restaurant on
the Missouri-Iowa border—that was halfway between
us—and I took the boys home with me. On Sunday afternoon we drove back to the border restaurant and Ken took
the boys home."

The plan worked for ten months, until Ken announced
he and the boys were moving to Houston. "That was the
end of weekends with my sons," Charlotte said. "It also

meant that I could never see them in plays or music recitals or baseball games. Visits required airplane flights, and that meant expensive tickets."

At first Charlotte was hurt and lonely, but soon she decided it might be a better plan after all. No longer was the boys' time with her made up of quick weekend visits and 250-mile drives each way. "When they came to see me, we really spent time together," Charlotte said. "I planned my life around the boys, and we really got to know each other."

Two years later, Charlotte married Spencer, a businessman with eleven-year-old twin girls and a six-year-old boy. "My boys moved up to live with us, and we had Spencer's children for eight weeks in the summer and every other weekend," Charlotte recalled. "It allowed us time to all be a family together."

Charlotte smiled when she remembered those special family times. "Every week we would have family marathon movie night," she recalled. "We would get a whole stack of videos, fill buckets with popcorn, pile pillows into our basement rec room, and watch movies from eight in the evening until ten or eleven the next morning. It was so much fun!"

Before Charlotte and Spencer were even married, they made a commitment to family. "We agreed that the best thing we could give our kids was ourselves. Since Spencer earned enough money for us to live on, we agreed I would be an at-home mom. If any child—mine or his—needed me at any time, I would be there for them. We went to the swimming pool and the golf course and made good use of the hiking trails. If someone was involved in an activity, we all went to cheer that person on. We loved baseball games, and we took family trips to other cities to see our favorite teams play. During our eight summer weeks together, we went on all kinds of mini-trips—and even a few maxi-trips!"

Then after five years, Charlotte and Spencer's marriage ended. "Everyone's life came crashing down,"

Charlotte said sadly. "When we told the girls, one of them said, 'So, then, that's the end of us and our family.' She was right."

GLIDING OUT A CHILD'S PAIN

Judith Wallerstein talks extensively about the "over-burdened" child. When a marriage breaks down, both mom and dad often find they cannot keep on parenting like they used to. Maybe they give less time. Maybe they let the discipline slide. Maybe they are so caught up in the storm of divorce and its aftermath that they're less sensitive to their children. Maybe they are afraid to be vulnerable again. Whatever the reason, parents are temporarily unable to separate their children's needs from their own.

"I knew the kids needed me," Charlotte said, "but it was all I could do to keep my own head above water."

Indeed. Wallerstein reports that a decade after the divorce, one-fourth of the ex-wives in her study and one-fifth of the ex-husbands still felt that life was unfair, disappointing, and lonely. This diminished capacity permanently disrupted the functioning of everyone involved. With parents disorganized and unable to meet the challenges before them, the children had to do whatever they could to keep their parents functioning.

"Looking back, I feel so bad," Charlotte said. "It was terribly unfair to push our kids into the position of having to rescue us. At the time I was helpless to do anything different, but in retrospect I can see what a burden it was on them. I had a driving need to prove to myself that I had indeed made a difference in the lives of my stepchildren. I pushed Maggie especially hard, because she was the oldest, and because she and I had been the closest. I called her on the telephone, I poured out my heart to her, I cried in front of her, I hinted and prodded and asked leading questions just to hear her say, 'I still love you,' and to call me 'Mom' once more."

But Maggie, just a junior in high school and struggling herself, felt trapped by Charlotte. As time went on and Charlotte pressed harder, Maggie finally reached the end of her patience. "Leave me alone!" she exploded one day after Charlotte had stopped by yet again. "If I want to see you, I'll call you. Until then, please, *please,* just leave me alone!"

Fully 15 percent of the children in Wallerstein's study were identified as "over-burdened" children.

Spencer was just the opposite. "When we were married, he was great to the kids," Charlotte said. "He loved sports, and he included the children in everything. He took them to games and patiently explained what was happening. Spencer was the judge of my oldest son's high school debate team and was involved in both boys' scout troops. But after the divorce, he dropped out of their lives completely. Two months later, my oldest son graduated from high school. Spencer was invited to the graduation ceremony, but he didn't come."

During the ceremony, Charlotte, with tears spilling from her eyes, whispered to her mother, "It's so sad. Spencer meant so much to Glen and contributed so much to his life. He should be here!"

Her mother replied, "It's his choice."

But what about Glen? What about Maggie and the other children? They were all deeply affected, yet they had no choice.

Spencer let Charlotte know she no longer had any responsibility for his children. Furthermore, he requested that she have no contact with them until the divorce was final. "But we agreed that neither of us should do anything to keep our kids apart," Charlotte said. "They were too important to each other."

That was a wise step. Children who have come to know each other as brothers and sisters should feel they are still included in major events in both houses. That takes some effort on the part of the parents. For instance, we plan Carley and Joanna's birthday parties with Nick and Brent's schedules in mind. It's important to them that the boys be here.

Inviting the children to be included doesn't mean insisting that they come. It means giving them a choice. When Nancy's family held their family reunion recently, we made sure both boys knew they were invited. Brent wanted to attend—it's his bloodline. But Nick, who wasn't related to anyone there, wasn't interested and decided not to come. That was fine. He knew the choice was his.

GLIDING OUT THE COMPETITION

Julia was so depressed that it was a struggle to get out of bed in the morning. Her problem? Her ex-husband had a new girlfriend.

"How can I compete with her?" Julia asked. "She's gorgeous, and look at me—I'm far from spectacular. She has a perfect figure, I'm dumpy and overweight. She's exciting, I'm boring. She has a great job, I clerk at the grocery store and struggle to pay the rent. How can I ever hope to compete with her?"

She can't. But fortunately for all of us, parenting isn't about competing. Julia has something on her side that the shapely, attractive, interesting person can never have. Julia is the children's mother. She is the one who nursed them through the chicken pox. She is the one who bandaged their skinned knees and made the hurt better with a kiss. She is the one who told them bedtime stories and rocked them back to sleep when they had bad dreams. She is the one who knows that Magic Mints are their favorite treat and always remembers to pick up a box when she goes to the grocery store. She is the one who drives them to track meets and sits on the cold cement bleachers for two hours so she will be there to cheer during the one sprint her child runs.

Do Julia's children love her because of her size or accomplishments? No! They love her because she is their mother.

No, Julia, you do not have to compete with this new person. All you have to do is be a loving, caring mom to your children.

"But that beautiful person wants to buy my children Christmas presents!" Julia exclaimed.

Great! Then the children will have one more interested person involved in their lives.

"But she's trying to buy their love!"

Let her be her. Let her have her relationship with the children and you go right on having yours. Have your children write nice thank-you notes for the gifts she buys. Speak courteously and politely to them about "Dad's new friend." If you can't think of anything nice to say, keep your mouth shut. That's the best thing you can do for your children and for your relationship with them. The worst thing you can do is make your children feel that any friendship with her means they are disloyal to you and that they will have to choose between you.

We realize it will be hard for Julia to do this. Perhaps it will be hard for you, too. A depressed parent, or one with low self-esteem, is less capable of handling these glitches. If you can't handle it, consult a professional who can help you get out of that place of desperation and move to a place where you can gain some perspective.

"But I can't do anything," you may say. "I have no skills."

Good news! An excellent resource, available in many areas throughout the country, is an organization called Women Work!, formerly known as Displaced Homemakers. Founded by the Junior League and usually located in conjunction with a community college, this national foundation makes it possible for a homemaker to receive the equivalent of $500 in occupational testing to determine her areas of interest, as well as to discover where her talents and abilities lie. She can also receive counseling to help raise her self-image so that she will be in a better position to get a job. The goal of the organization is to give people like Julia direction in life. It helps get their focus off their problems and gets them into the work place. It shows them they are valuable people who have something to offer society. For more information on this organization, contact:

Women Work! The National Network for Women's Employment
1625 K Street NW, Suite 300
Washington, D.C. 20006
Telephone: (202) 467-6346
FAX: (202) 467-5366

"I didn't feel I *had* to compete," Marianne confessed. "I *wanted* to compete, because I wanted to prove myself the winner. When my girls were getting ready to go to their father's house, I would tell them, 'Don't you let that woman brush your hair. You brush each other's hair. She is not your mother, and don't you forget it!'"

Marianne thought she was hurting her husband and his new wife. She wasn't. She was hurting her children.

GLIDING OUT THE GLITCH OF CHANGE

"So how exactly do I go about gliding out the glitches?" you may be asking. Here are some specific techniques that have been helpful to many.

Be willing to ask your ex-spouse for forgiveness. Yes, you read that right. If something you have done is causing friction, be willing to apologize.

"But what if I'm not completely wrong?" you ask.

So what? You can still say, "I truly am sorry that this has hurt you. I don't want to cause you more pain. Please forgive me." Your graciousness will raise you in that other person's esteem, and it will make a real difference for your child.

Think mediation before litigation. Once you get on the

litigation track, you will find it very hard to get off. After litigation, the wounds are so deep that having any kind of parenting relationship with your ex-spouse can be tough. Sure, there are touchy issues between you two parents. And we understand that if you don't have a good parenting relationship, trying to work those issues out alone may just make you angrier and more resentful. We suggest you look for a caring, knowledgeable person who can assist you. If the issue has to do with school, perhaps the school counselor would be a good choice. Or maybe a counselor at church could help, or a professional counselor or mediator.

Do as many things right as you possibly can. You are going to mess up now and then. Everyone does. We've certainly made our share of blunders. That's why it's so important for all of us to build up a huge backlog of good, generous, thoughtful actions. That way, when you blow it, your mistake will be far outweighed by all the things you have done right.

Take the initiative and be creative. We know how much easier it is to sit and complain about the trials of your situation than it is to takes steps toward fixing them. But we will assure you of one thing: If you don't take the initiative to do something to make it better, no one will. You say your kids are too far away for you to have continual input into their lives? Take the initiative! Telephone them regularly, perhaps every night, to say, "Good night, I love you." A five-minute call after five o'clock won't be that expensive. Or check out some children's books from the library and read them onto tape so your kids can hear a bedtime story from you. Or make them video tapes of yourself reading a picture book or playing with your dog or flying a model airplane. Encourage them to send you a video of themselves.

Be as fair as you can possibly be. We know, we know — life isn't fair. We probably say that to ourselves, each other, and our kids twenty times a day. And it's true. But we can still aim to make life as fair as we possibly can. Each of the children in your family, regardless of how he got there, wants to know he is as important to the family and as valuable to you as any other child. This equal acceptance is something we have discussed before, but we want to remind you again. It is so vital. Continue to strive toward it.

We've made super efforts on behalf of Brent and Nick, since each is the stepson of one of us. For instance, in appreciation of Nick's musical interest, Nancy went to a music store going out of business and saw a wonderful fiberglass saxophone priced at $500. Every week she went back and checked the newly reduced price. When it got down to $60, she bought the sax as a Christmas present for Nick.

Don't confuse *fair* with *equal*, however. One woman who had both a biological daughter and a stepdaughter was so determined to keep things equal that when her daughter got a $110 formal for the senior prom, mom insisted her younger stepdaughter also buy an item of clothing for $110. Everyone ended up angry and resentful. Her husband was furious that their already strained budget had been blown, the oldest daughter resented the intrusion on her special day, and the stepdaughter was upset because later, when she wanted to go on a class trip, she was told, "Sorry, we don't have any more money for you."

Things are never going to be truly fair. We once got Brent a camera at a garage sale in Atlanta. It was worth $1500 and we paid $300. We didn't get such an expensive gift for any of the other children.

Being fair means treating each child as a worthwhile individual. Sometimes the best gestures cost very little. When Brent was eleven, Nancy sent a letter to the Orlando Magic basketball team and arranged for him to be a ball boy on the night of his birthday! That wouldn't have meant much to Nick, who was much more into cars.

But Nancy happened to have a client who owned a $300,000 Lamborghini, and she arranged for him to give Nick a ride in his car for Nick's birthday. To Nick, that was impressive!

Resist the temptation to second-guess. Laura's stepson was an extremely intelligent boy who had always excelled in school. When he turned fourteen, his face began to break out, his voice cracked, he began to notice girls, and his grades plummeted. "Eleanor, his mother, was convinced the changes in him were caused by something we were doing wrong," Laura said. "She asked, 'Have you had him tested for drugs? Have you checked his room for alcohol? Is he listening to heavy metal music? What kind of friends are you letting him run around with?'"

Certainly there are kids who get into trouble, and there are kids who are able to hide some pretty serious things from their parents. And certainly changes in behavior need to be taken seriously, and in some instances, investigated. But second-guessing the other family and accusing them of negligence is extremely frustrating, not to mention totally unfair.

Eleanor refused to communicate with her ex-husband, only with Laura. Laura told her, "Look, Eleanor, we are doing everything we know to do." But Eleanor was still unhappy. Finally, in exasperation, Laura told her, "If you think you can do a better job, Gary and I are willing to let the boy move in with you." Immediately, Eleanor backed off.

Work out a schedule agreeable to everyone. Most people think of traditional every-other-weekend type schedules. But work together with your ex-spouse and come up with one that will best fit the needs of all. Some dates you might want to consider: holidays, the child's birthday, parents' birthdays, Mother's Day, Father's Day. You will also want to think about the business travel requirements (or opportunities) of one parent or the other, school holidays, vacations, transportation responsibilities, sibling considerations, school, and extra-curricular considerations.

Little Freddie spends Thanksgiving with mom and Christmas with dad one year. The next year he spends Thanksgiving with dad and Christmas with mom. He also alternates birthdays, summer vacation, Labor Day, and Memorial Day. Sounds fair, doesn't it? We used to think so, but we've changed our minds. The reason? It's awfully hard to build traditions in the absence of continuity.

Family traditions are so important. We all love looking forward to doing things the way they are always done. It feels comfortable and secure. It's far easier to do that when special days are consistent and predictable. Decide how you can divide up special times so your child can build traditions with both your family and the family of your ex-spouse.

"Every Thanksgiving, we go to Grandma's house in the desert," little Freddie can say. "My cousins and uncles and aunts and everyone play football in the back yard before dinner. We kids get to eat at a special table of our own. We laugh and play and talk with our mouths full and no adults tell us to mind our manners. If we get too noisy, they just move our table out onto the back porch."

And he can say, "Christmas with my dad is so cool. We get up really, really early in the morning and sneak down to look at our presents. We make lots of noise so Dad and Mary have to get up. After we open our presents, we cook a huge breakfast, and we get to play with our new toys for as long as we want. It's so cool!"

You might say, "We had some pretty great traditions in our old family. My kids still talk longingly about them." Maybe you can hold onto those old traditions. However, since you are blending two families, you will likely have to do some adjusting. Let's say you always had an all-out camping trip on Labor Day, but now your ex gets the kids for Labor Day. Well, why not move your camping trip to Memorial Day or the Fourth of July? It could be your new family's tradition. You might even decide to include some of the kids from your children's extended family.

And there are other benefits of consistently having the children on specific dates. If your friends and relatives know you never have them on Labor Day but always on Memorial Day, for instance, they can plan special outings—even a family reunion—for that holiday.

Certainly you need to be flexible. But keep in mind that structure and predictability are very important to kids. In fact, we suggest you get each child a calendar for each home. Fill it in with special days throughout the year—family birthdays, other special family celebrations, activities that affect your child. Not only is it good for the child, but it lets stepbrothers and stepsisters know when that child will be around their house.

It is unlikely that any of you is going to get your first choice of everything. Be willing to give and take.

Stay in control. How can you remain patient, kind, loving, and dependable at all times? You probably can't. We know we can't. Don't strive for perfection. Strive to stay in control.

To Laura's horror, Eleanor gave her son a Christmas gift of a set of drums. The boy came home, set the drums up in the middle of the living room, and began to practice with great enthusiasm. He practiced all day, and the next day, and the next and the next and the next. By the end of the week, Laura and Gary thought they would lose their minds.

"We lived in a small house, and the living room was the only place where we could all relax together. Those drums took up more than half the floor space," Laura said. "And believe me, you can't sit and watch television or listen to the stereo or have a conversation while someone is in there playing the drums!"

Gary and Laura decided their son had a choice: He could either keep the drums in his room or he could keep them at his mother's house.

"I want them here," he insisted, "and there's not enough room in my bedroom."

"Then something will have to go from your bedroom," Laura said.

The drums went into his room. He also abided by the drumming hours his parents posted. Through it all, Gary and Laura stayed in control.

Instead of two houses, let your children have two homes. If your children have to carry a suitcase from one house to another, they will feel like visitors. If they have a closet with their own clothes hanging in it and a bed with their own stuffed animals on it, they will feel at home. Be sure your children have their own belongings in both houses so that both houses will be home.

"Hold it!" you may be saying. "We can't afford to buy two of everything."

No? Not even if you shop at thrift stores or garage sales? Not even if you allow some of the things you buy to go to the other house? Not even if you divide up what they already own between the two houses? Not even when you understand how important it is to make your children feel at home?

Respect the privacy of others. You may get really curious about what is going on in your ex-spouse's home. How do they live? What do they do in the evenings? Do any of your old friends drop by for a visit? Have they bought any expensive things lately? When your children come home from their time at the other house, it's tempting to pump them. *Don't do it.* That family is entitled to privacy boundaries just as your family is.

"Hey," you may say. "If they want to know anything about me, let them ask. I don't have any secrets."

Certainly, some people are more private than others. But private or not, your children should never be put in the position of having to act as spies. Respect their rights to privacy, too.

"I don't have to ask the kids anything," you may say.

"They are absolute chatterboxes. They walk in the door talking."

Then maybe you need to discuss the idea of privacy with them. It's important that your children understand what is appropriate to share and what isn't. If there is no benefit to a piece of information, if it hurts someone, or if it invades another's privacy, it should not be shared.

WHEN YOU CAN'T GLIDE

"My biggest challenge was fear that my ex-husband was too lenient about what he allowed in his home," Nancy admits. "For instance, I didn't want Brent watching movies we didn't allow."

Like it or not, none of us can police what goes on in the other household. What you can do is your absolute best to teach your children right from wrong. Instead of trying to enforce a list of do's and don'ts, demonstrate your value system by the way you live, and let the kids know the reasons behind your beliefs.

"I don't know," you may be saying. "I think my glitches may run too deep for these measures."

Then we suggest you consider professional help.

PROFESSIONAL HELP
It's time to seek professional help when

- ❖ troubled behavior persists in your child for longer than a month or two;
- ❖ your child's behavior is consistently below what is appropriate for his age;
- ❖ her low self-esteem is reflected in self-neglect or self-injury;
- ❖ a physical pattern or motion is repeated compulsively;
- ❖ he is either unable to play alone or will only play alone;

❖ there is a sudden change in behavior that inter-
   feres with day-to-day living;
❖ your child suffers ongoing pain that has no
   obvious physical origin;
❖ he is consistently aggressive in his behavior;
❖ she falls apart every time she makes a mistake;
❖ your child is just too good to be true.

HELPING OUR LAMBS

If a sheep falls down it can't get up by itself. Sheep legs
can't manage it. On its back, a sheep can only live for five
hours. That's why shepherds check their sheep regularly.
Parents are a lot like shepherds. If our children stumble
and fall, they can't get up by themselves. And so we need
continually to check to see that they are on their feet. If
not, it is up to us to help them tenderly back up.

Our children want to know we care, yet they hate to
be smothered. It's a tough balance for parents to strike.
Now and then when our Joanna doesn't get her way, she
stomps her feet and exclaims, "Then I'll just go back to
my Romanian mommy!"

Sometimes we're tempted to shoot back, "Oh, sure,
that mom who mistreated and neglected you. That mom
who was never there for you." But we don't. We bite our
tongues and do our best to get her back on her feet.

There are times when we, too, fall down and can't get
up. Our children are well aware of what we do then—
we call on God to help us back onto our feet. Our children have seen us cry. They've heard us say, "I was
wrong. I'm sorry." And they have heard us pray for the
strength we don't have and the wisdom we lack. By letting them see us as we really are, we're teaching them to
glide out their own glitches.

Chapter Nine

IT'S NEVER TOO LATE

How to Get on Track When Things Are a Mess

Connie and Wayne have done everything wrong. Connie has steadfastly refused to speak with her ex in any way, at any time, about anything. As for Wayne, whenever he and his ex were in the same room, they would argue and insult and berate each other. In their home together, Connie and Wayne disagreed on just about everything—the children's behavior, whose discipline methods were best, what the house rules should be, how much Wayne was overpaying in child support.

"Our family is really hurting," Connie admits. "If only we'd had some help when we were first starting out in our blended family, maybe then we could have done things better. But everything is so bad now, I guess it's too late for us."

Perhaps you are feeling the same way. Maybe your family, too, started out all wrong. By now, you may be well into the process of being a family, but it's not turning out the way you had planned. You've been reading this book and saying, "That's all well and good for those families who are just starting out, but what about the rest of us? Is it too late for us?"

It is never too late. Don't waste time lamenting what you have or haven't done. Pat Williams, general manager of the Orlando Magic basketball team, said, "People who succeed use the past as a springboard rather than a hammock." That's a good rule for all of us.

The perfect time to get out of your hammock and move your family onto the right track is now.

"But how should I start?" you may be asking.

First, sit down with your spouse and talk. Agree that from this moment on the two of you will work in unison and let the children know there will be no division between you. Agree that you will deal with any disagreements behind closed doors, when the children are out of earshot. Then make a list of the areas in which you would most like to see changes in your family.

The next step is to go to your respective ex-spouses (or write a letter if that would work better). You might say something such as, "Look, neither you nor I had any training in parenting. We just stumbled along doing the best we could. I've been doing some reading and research, and I realize I've made mistakes. I'd like to share with you some of the ideas I've read that I think might help all of us. Could we get together and talk about these things?" This approach is a good one, because you are not making judgments or casting blame on your ex-spouse. From there you can address some of the things we have discussed so far: coming up with a workable plan for communicating with each other, working together to share parenting in the best possible way, keeping your conflicts away from the kids, determining not to run each other down in front of the children, and putting your children's welfare ahead of your anger and bitterness.

Certainly you will not be able to make sweeping changes all at once. In some areas, deep change may not even be realistic. Perhaps all you can hope for is a degree of modification.

Then again, maybe not. You won't know until you try.

BUT OUR KIDS ARE ALMOST GROWN

It was Jennifer's wedding day. She stood at the back of the church, her maid of honor fussing with the satin and lace wedding gown, her bridesmaids fixing the flowers in her hair and touching up her lipstick. Suddenly Jennifer pulled away and rushed to the back door. Her agitation growing, she paced back and forth, back and forth.

"What's wrong, Jen?" her maid of honor asked.

"I can't do it!" Jennifer said. "I can't go through with this!" She rushed out the back door, leaving her shocked attendants staring after her. The wedding was off.

"I couldn't go through with it," Jennifer later explained. "All I could think of was, what if my marriage ends like my parents'? What if I become as angry and bitter as my mother? I couldn't run the risk of having to endure the pain they have endured, and I couldn't condemn my children to the agony I have known."

Pretty drastic response, you say? Yes, it is. But it happened. More than once we have seen children utterly destroyed by their parents' pain. Perhaps the most extreme examples have come from juvenile court where we deal with kids who feel emotionally abandoned by their warring parents. These are the kids who end up on the streets, in gangs, in trouble with the law. Not finding the emotional support they need at home, they turn to their peers—or to alcohol or drugs.

Whatever your children's ages, don't write off your responsibility to them. You always have an opportunity to make a difference in their lives. If it's too hard to think about the long term, take it on a day-by-day basis. Each night as you go to sleep, say: *This is what I did today. This is what I am going to do tomorrow.*

"Hold it! That means communication."

We know. The big 'C' word again.

"After all this time, we won't be able to do it," you say.

You must.

"We've tried and it doesn't work."

Force yourself. It's true that starting to communicate now is not going to be easy. Any time we are required to relearn something, we don't do as well as we did the first time around. But we *can* relearn. And in the case of communication, it is an essential. Perhaps it would help to go back to Chapter 3 and review the various stages of communication.

And, please, don't let the initial discomfort stop you. Think of it as diving into a cool swimming pool on a hot day. You know it is going to be okay once you get in, but you dread that first shock of cold water. Yet you are never going to be able to enjoy that refreshing swim unless you first dive in and suffer for a few moments. It will be the same with starting to communicate. You have to take that initial plunge.

TALK TO YOUR KIDS

You say you don't have the privilege of shared parenting? That you are limited to weekend "visitation"? Then look for other ways to let your children know you are thinking of them daily. Call them on a regular basis. If they are younger than eight years old, you might call every couple of days. You don't want to be intrusive to their other family, so you might want to clear it with them first. For instance, you could say, "I would like to call on Tuesday and Thursday evenings at eight o'clock. I'll keep the conversation short—no more than five minutes."

You can tell older children they are welcome to call you at any time (or within certain time limits, if that works better for you). Then you can limit your calls to them to special occasions ("I've been thinking about you today. How did the history report go?").

CUT THE SUBLIMINAL COMMUNICATION

Your words may not be what is causing trouble. It may be what's behind those words that's the problem. We sometimes convince ourselves that our anger and bitterness aren't harmful to our children if they seep through disguised as "innocent" comments. ("Your father was always so busy working that he never had time for us.")

Don't be fooled; subliminal messages are exceedingly dangerous. And if you find yourself sending them, do whatever it takes to stop.

BECOME A GOOD LISTENER

One of the biggest problems in families that aren't working well is that everyone wants to talk and no one wants to listen. You can start the healing process by learning to listen. Need help? Here are ten ways to improve your listening skills.

1. *Listen with purpose.*

   When you speak, you have a purpose for what you say. It should be the same with your listening. Ask yourself: What is my reason for listening? Is it to understand the other person's message? Is it to try to learn her motivation or to assess his credibility? Is it to feel what the other person is feeling?

2. *Accept that the other person has something worthwhile to say.*

   If you look at listening to that other person as a way of working together as a team, it will help you see its importance.

3. *Care about the other person.*

   Show your concern for the other person's problems and issues. A caring person is a good listener.

4. *Be sensitive to the speaker's situation.*

   Listening to your stepchild is different from listening to your birth child. Listening to your ex-spouse is different from listening to your present spouse. Listening to your ex-spouse's new spouse is different from any other situation. Be sensitive to the point of view of the person speaking.

5. *Know your emotional triggers.*

   What words set you off? An effective listener knows that certain words, phrases, and topics create strong and often irrational feelings that may be

difficult to control. Steer the conversation away
from these triggers.

6. *Concentrate on the other person's message.*
   Do the person's words fit the nonverbal message
   she is sending? What does his message say about
   his attitude toward you, his determination to take
   action, or his emotional stability?

7. *Restate the message to ensure you understand what the
   other person is saying.*
   You might say something such as: "What I hear you
   saying is that you feel your dad and I have different
   expectations for you and that his are more realistic
   than mine. Is that correct?" Restating allows you to
   determine if what you think that person is saying is
   what he thinks he's saying.

8. *Allow your knowledge of the person, the family, and the
   background circumstances to help you understand what
   the other person is saying.*
   Considering everything you know about the situation, is what you are hearing logical? Is this the kind
   of statement you would expect from this person?

9. *Get organized!*
   Write down important things you hear, such as
   dates to remember ("The school play tryouts are
   next Friday at four o'clock. I want to go"). Make a
   mental note of your child's concerns or fears ("I'm
   really worried about having to play basketball in
   P.E. I'm no good at it and no one wants me on their
   team"), plans for future action ("When I'm at
   Mom's house next weekend, I'm going to ask her if
   I can spend more time over there"), and questions
   that remain unanswered ("I don't know what I
   want to do next year. I'm really confused").

10. *Know your listening limits.*
    You cannot be at your best all the time. Be sensitive
    to your internal, emotional, psychological, and
    physical condition. Schedule important listening

responsibilities for times when you are most prepared to meet those responsibilities. ("What you're saying is really important to me, but I'm so tired I can't give you the attention you deserve. Can we talk after dinner?")

Good listeners are hard to come by. You can be one for your family.

NO MORE UNDERMINING

If a pattern of undermining one another has built up in your family, break it now. Here are some mistakes parents commonly make.

Listening in on children's telephone calls. Kids should not feel that one parent is eavesdropping while they talk to their other parent. If you are listening in on telephone calls, stop it. And stop quizzing the children afterward about who said what. If you need to know something, ask the adult involved—your ex-spouse, for instance. Actually, this can be a pretty good measuring stick. If you don't need to know, you will probably be too embarrassed to ask!

Don't commit someone else to anything without his or her permission. We never cease to be amazed that a parent can sign a child up for an activity that requires a commitment of time and money from the other parent without ever discussing it with that other parent.

When Nick was young, he begged his mother to let him get into dirt bike competition. Before his mother approved, she asked Bill's opinion. After all, we would have to get Nick to competitions on the weekends he was with us, and we would also have to pay the entry fees on those days. Nancy wasn't excited about it; Carley was little, and dirt bike tracks are not the nicest places for little ones to run around. But Nick really did enjoy the sport, so one or the other of us made it a point to be there with him. Sometimes we all went and made it a family time.

We would have felt a whole lot different about the situation had Nick's mom signed him up without first discussing it with us.

ADJUST TO DIFFERENCES

"I'll admit I'm at war with my ex," Victoria told us, "but there is no way to avoid it. My husband and I have made a commitment to certain values, and we feel that discipline is important. But my ex-spouse's family is totally different. When the children are over there, anything goes. It just isn't acceptable to us."

Unless there is real neglect or some sort of abuse going on, Victoria has no say over her ex-husband's parenting methods. Sure, it's great if the two families can agree on their approaches to parenting, but if not, you will have to adjust. Your children can do it, and they will, if you don't make a big problem out of it.

She believes in spanking, he doesn't. She insists on apologies from the children for their wrongdoing, he shrugs his shoulders and says, "Kids will be kids." She punishes the children for using off-color words or comments, he encourages them by laughing.

If you don't agree on parenting, the best thing you can do is continue doing what you think is best and hold your tongue about the other family. If your children complain, explain, "I'm sorry if you are unhappy, but this is how we do it in our family. I love you very much, and I am doing what I feel is best for you."

Perhaps through mutual compromise your families can come closer together on parenting practices. For instance, if you both agree to ignore the naughty words, your child may well lose interest in them. What's the use if he can't upset his mom or make his dad laugh?

"But what if the differences aren't just between the two families?" you may say. "What if they are here in my own home?"

We have talked about the importance of presenting a united front, but we also know that if facing off against each other is your pattern, it might be hard to change. If you just can't seem to find any middle ground, and if you feel the issue is too important for compromise, it may be time to seek help from a professional.

WHEN YOU NEED MORE HELP

"Marianne and I had a lot in common," Nancy says of her long-time friend. "Both our husbands had left us for younger women. We struggled to get by as single moms as we worked our way through law school. We were both bitter and resentful."

But Marianne refused to let go of her bitterness. She resented every minute of contact her daughters had with her ex-husband, and she never missed a chance to take a verbal swipe at him in her girls' presence.

"In time I had to sit down with my friend and tell her in love, 'Marianne, you can't keep on doing this to your girls,'" Nancy says.

"I know," Marianne replied. "I realize I'm hurting them, but I can't do anything about it. I just can't stand to see my daughters with that man who betrayed all of us. And it kills me to think of them being *mothered* by that girl he married. I just can't stand it!"

Marianne's bitterness was destroying her, and it was destroying her children as well. If she had remarried and started a new family while this was still boiling inside her, it would likely have destroyed that new family, too. Fortunately, that didn't happen.

Marianne realized she needed professional help. She was six months into her first job and was pleased to discover that her health insurance would help cover mental health costs.

"My ex-husband should be here," Marianne told the therapist on their first session together.

"No, he shouldn't," she replied.

"Now wait just a minute!" Marianne protested. "He was the unfaithful jerk who started this whole thing!"

"I'm not suggesting he wasn't wrong," the therapist answered. "But we are here to work on you, not him."

You say your ex is the problem? Or your present spouse? Or maybe your children or your stepchildren? No matter. You make the move to get help for yourself. Your therapist can identify the other people who need to participate. Willingness to step out—even if you stand alone at first—presents a model the others in your family can follow. If you are willing to say you are ashamed of some of your past behaviors and are doing your best to correct them, it will be easier for others to come along in your footsteps and do the same. Peace in your family can begin with you.

The same counseling professional may not be right for everyone. Some will only feel comfortable with a counselor who shares their particular religious faith. Others will want only a woman (or a man) or a counselor who is himself in a blended family. Some may respond better to someone who is of their ethnic background.

For instance, Dr. Charles English, a psychotherapist from Winter Park, Florida, is developing a specific approach for multicultural counseling. "Most counseling theories are based upon Euro-centric models," Dr. English says. "There is little consideration given to African-centric, or Asian or Hispanic counseling. It's a new area, particularly in terms of practice. I tell the students in my classes that when you go to a person's office, you can tell which culture that person holds in esteem. I try to create a healing ambiance, and I think my clients feel that. Not only do I minister to their behavior, but I also take into consideration the African-centric notion of healing the spirit and soul."

Carefully consider the specific needs of your family. Get references from your physician or pediatrician, or from friends or relatives who have been in counseling.

When you call the counselor, ask for a get-acquainted meeting (sometimes you can do this by telephone). Your questions should include:

✤ What is your training?

✤ Do you have a license? What is it in?

✤ How long have you been practicing?

✤ What has been your primary area of work?

✤ How much experience do you have in the specific concerns facing my family?

You may be saying, "Oh, I can't afford that!"

No? Your family's health is worth a lot. Check your medical insurance and see what it covers in this area. If your policy limits you to a clinic that is not your first choice, yet you feel you can't afford anything else, go for it. Something is better than nothing.

Many churches, and the Jewish Social Services, offer counseling. The Catholic church has a national program for children of divorce called Rainbows. Start looking and asking.

NEVER TOO LATE?

The four children in Quentin and Joy's blended family are basically grown; the youngest is in his third year of college four states away.

"They don't think we did such a good job with them," Joy admitted. "Just last week one daughter called and said, 'You were so worried about making each other happy, you had no time for us.'"

"I can't believe some of the things we did," Quentin added sadly. "Joy and I actually went away together on our first Christmas and left the kids to fend for themselves! Our feeling was, *We will only have them a few yea·s, but we will have us forever.* It's true, but we should have centered those first few years on them."

"The kids hold a lot of resentments toward us," Joy said. "What can we do?"

They can begin by telling their children, "I'm sorry." If they can't do it in person, they can do it in writing. They can apologize to each child individually and specifically. They can tell each child how important he or she is to them, and they can look for ways to demonstrate it. If the distance will allow it, they might invite their children to join them in counseling sessions where all are free to express themselves.

Even though you made mistakes, you surely didn't do *everything* wrong. Let your children know you will rejoice in the parenting positives they learned from you and will practice in their own families. Also let them know you respect the lessons they learned from the mistakes you made.

Perhaps Joy and Quentin can take heart from Paula. She was an angry, screaming mother who couldn't get rid of her bitterness. But as a grandmother, Paula realized how inappropriate and damaging her behavior had been.

"I asked my children to come for Thanksgiving one year," she said. "One daughter was especially hard to convince, but in the end they all made it. I told them all how much I love them, and had a personal letter for each child. I asked for their forgiveness for my foolish behavior. And I asked them to please give me another chance in the lives of my grandchildren. There were a lot of tears shed that night, and a lot of fences were mended. I am proud to say, my children are better parents than I ever was."

No, it's never too late.

A BETTER TOMORROW

At the time of our divorces, we were both educated people. We were both decent and caring, and we were loving parents. Yet we had no idea how to be divorced parents. We had to learn by trial and error—and there were more than a few errors.

Most parents truly want to do right by their children. The problem is, they don't know what to do. One of our goals is to see parenting programs available to all divorced parents throughout the country.

The first parenting program was mandated in the state of Kansas in 1986. Since 1990 there has been an explosion of parent education programs. These programs tend to focus on the needs of the children. An Association of Family and Conciliation Courts' survey at the University of Western Michigan found that although 90 percent of the participants in the survey stated they had initially resisted taking the course, afterward 90 percent recommended the course to others and 70 percent said the course should be mandatory. A study in Utah showed similar results: 80 percent of the people resented being required to come to a program, yet 90 percent of those who resisted said they came out with something positive.

What are your goals for your family? Write them down. Determine that tomorrow you will be closer to those goals than you are today, that one week from now you will be even closer, that one month from now you will be closer still.

If you have the determination and are willing to make the effort, it is never too late to move your family toward greater emotional health and happiness.

Chapter 10

CHILDHOOD
AND BEYOND

*Anticipating and Addressing the Problems
Your Kids May Have As They Grow Up*

"**P**ersonally, I think you make too much out of blended family difficulties," Marcy told us. "I mean, sure there are problems in blended families. But then there are problems in *any* family. I mean, so many kids are affected by divorce these days, and most of them are doing just fine."

To some degree, Marcy is right. All families *do* have problems. And since the average length of a marriage in our society today is seven years, it is also true that many children are affected by divorce. Of those children, nearly half have not seen their fathers within the year. What *isn't* true is that most of those children are doing just fine. If you doubt it, take a look at your newspaper and turn on the evening news. *Don't worry, everything will work out in time* is a dangerous attitude for the parent of a blended family.

A father, trying to keep his son occupied, took out a map of the world and made a puzzle out of it by ripping it in pieces. "Now," the dad said, "let's see you put this back together."

Five minutes later the boy was back. To his father's

astonishment, the map was reassembled perfectly.

"How did you do it so fast?" the dad asked.

"It was easy," the boy replied. "There was a picture of a boy riding his horse on the other side, so I put that picture together and then I turned it over. Once the boy was together, the world was back together, too."

That's the way we need to look at our kids. If we can keep them together emotionally, physically, and spiritually, everything else will work out.

"We can't protect our kids against everything," Marcy insisted. "They are going to have to handle the ups and downs of life, so they may as well start handling it now."

Right again. People who try to build a wall around their children to protect them from everything do the kids no favor. Kids must be given a chance to learn and to grow. We parents have to use wisdom, but we also have to let our children take risks. We need to allow them to gain experience from the outside world and to learn from their mistakes.

And yet we have to understand what is at stake for our kids. Our approaches to their needs, and our actions on their behalf, go far beyond childhood. Problems associated with divorce or death, and the blending of a new family, often remain under the surface until the children are grown and ready to enter into their own adult male-female relationships. This is referred to as the "sleeper effect."

Some of the areas in which long-term problems are most likely to show up are in the children's self-esteem, in their own adult intimate relationships, and in their own approaches to parenting.

SELF-ESTEEM

We all carry a picture of ourselves in our head. To us, that picture is reality. If it depicts us as strong and capable and attractive and intelligent, that's how we see ourselves. If it depicts us as weak and clumsy and homely and stupid, that's how we see ourselves. And we usually do an excellent job of living up or down to that picture.

If we keep our children in an atmosphere of inner pain, if we show by our actions that their welfare takes second place to our anger, if we demonstrate hatred for a part of them by hating their other parent, if the effort to smoothly blend our family is too much trouble to us, we are helping to paint some terrible things into our children's mental pictures of themselves.

As children grow toward adulthood, they progress through various stages of development, each with its own needs and lessons to be learned. If the pressures on a child at a certain age cause him to miss the lessons of that stage, it can affect him for life. Perhaps it will help you to understand how this works if we look at the highlights of each stage of development as laid out by Deborah O. Day, Psy.D., of Winter Park, Florida.

DEVELOPMENTAL STAGES

6-18 months

Such young children are very dependent on their parents. It is essential that they have a continued sense of trust, security, and confidence that their needs will be met. They also need a safe environment in which to explore and grow and learn. Predictability and familiarity are important to them. Children of this age strongly fear the loss of their primary caregiver and will be quite threatened if they are taken out of their familiar, comfortable, and predictable home.

Both parents need to have a great deal of patience with these little ones. They need to be sensitive to the issues in their children's young lives, such as the pain of teething, ear infections, and the struggle to take their first steps.

Meeting the needs of these young children takes commitment on the part of both parents. While it's important to have one primary residence, the nonresidential parent should have short, frequent visits, perhaps even daily.

18 months-3 years

This is the age at which children separate from their parents and begin to develop an independent sense of themselves. They have a driving desire to explore the world and the things in it. Since they are also constantly testing limits and seeking boundaries, firm, consistent, fair limits are essential. It's important that mom and dad be patient, predictable, loving, affectionate, and encouraging.

By this age, children are able to spend time away from their primary home for reasonable periods of time. They need both parents in their lives in order to maintain their sense of trust, security, confidence, and of being loved. Unless it is absolutely necessary, these little ones should not be separated from either parent for more than three days and nights.

Parents need to continue to be sensitive to their children's anxieties and any difficulties that come with change. You know special support is needed when you see your little ones demonstrate excessive aggression, severe separation fears, significantly delayed speech or regression in walking, frequent temper tantrums, or when development lags.

3-5 years

During these preschool years, children begin to develop their gender identity. They also learn to tell right from wrong, to earn the approval of others, and to control themselves. And they are learning about friendships.

You can help your preschooler adapt to the change between homes by prominently displaying photos of both parents in his or her room in each home. Also, both parents can make audiotapes of themselves reading favorite stories so mommy or daddy will both be close by, no matter which home the child is in. Encourage your child to take a favorite toy or object (blanket, stuffed animal, pillow, doll) along when he goes to the other house.

Parents should work together to develop a child's daily routine for sleeping, eating, and play time that everyone can live with. Then agree to adhere consistently to this schedule in both homes. Also, decide on similar discipline strategies and be consistent about applying them.

It's easy for parents to assume that children this age are too young to know what is going on between them. Please understand that these kids not only notice what you say, they notice what you do. Make it a rule to act pleasant around your ex. Because young children often feel responsible for their parents' divorce, they need lots of love and reassurance from both parents. Children of this age do best if they are allowed to see each parent every two or three days.

Signs that your preschooler needs special support are persistent sleep problems or changes in eating habits, a return to babyish behavior, changes in mood (becoming withdrawn or appearing depressed, losing interest in activities previously enjoyed, extended crying after separating from one parent, becoming unusually demanding and needy, becoming uncharacteristically wild and out of control).

6 years

In order to cope with school demands, to develop good feelings about their ability to work and play cooperatively with other children, six-year-olds need to feel free from family worries. They are developing their ability to think logically now and are beginning to understand the concept of fairness. Children of this age feel good about themselves when they achieve success in school, in extracurricular activities, and through friendships.

Continue to stick to the daily schedule and be consistent in your discipline. Agree with your ex on which chores are appropriate for your child, and make two copies of chore reminder charts so one can be posted at each home. This will help develop good work habits in your child. Also, communicate closely with each other about homework assignments and notices from school.

At this age the actual parenting schedule—which days the child is with you and which days he is with his other parent—is not as important to his adjustment as making sure he feels free to love both parents while experiencing as little conflict between them as possible. If you have a successful, well-established parenting schedule, continue with it.

Besides the concerns already mentioned, special support is needed when you see problems with your child's behavior or academic achievement at school, or if she is becoming intensely angry with the parent she blames for the divorce. If the child's anger is allowed to continue, it can result in rejecting that parent and refusing to spend time with him or her. It is a problem if your child either becomes unrealistically cheerful and denies that there are any problems at all or if she becomes too serious.

7-8 years
At this age, children are "branching out" from their parents. More and more of their time is spent in school, with hobbies, with friends, and in various activities.

The majority of these kids are still harboring the hope that mom and dad will get back together. Your child may even attempt to reunite you. Many also are filled with sadness and a fear of losing both parents.

While these children need both their parents and are able to move between the two homes with minimal stress, they also have a strong need for a "home base" where they can make friends, get involved in community activities, and feel secure.

You know special support is needed when the child is preoccupied with divorce, academic problems, or sadness.

9-10 years

At this age, kids are part children and part independent thinkers. They are no longer as prone to fantasize about getting their parents back together. In fact, if their minds have not been too manipulated by one parent or the other, they have some empathy for each. Their friends are important to them, but their parents are still more important. They want both their parents to watch them play basketball, dance in the ballet recital, or sing in the church musical. And they want both parents to know their coaches and teachers.

Children at this age are likely to ask questions about the divorce: "Why did you and Daddy get a divorce?" "Why don't you love Mommy any more?" They want to be reassured they still belong, there is stability in their home base, and they will continue to see both their parents regularly.

11-12 years

Friends are becoming more important to children of this age. In fact, a close friend may be more of a confidant now than either parent. These children's needs for security and belonging, and for positive self-esteem, continue to come largely from their family, but also come from friends and school and athletic pursuits.

The conscience is more developed now, and these children respond to the emotions of others. They are well able to discuss issues, and they want explanations. Don't be surprised if they have more to say about the divorce, and if they make moral judgments. In fact, these kids may know much more about the issues between their parents than the parents realize.

For these pre-adolescents, feelings can be fragile. If they are pushed away by their peers, they may feel unloved. They may also feel a sense of rage or betrayal about the divorce and pronounce, "It's all your fault!" to the parent they feel abandoned them. Many demonstrate their rage by allying themselves with the other parent.

Kids this age need special support when they are put in the position of having to care for younger children of the family or when they have to be the emotional support for their parents. Other areas of concern are frequent acting up in school, aggressiveness, and anger directed toward one or both parents. If an eleven- or twelve-year-old shows signs of depression or threatens suicide, it should definitely be taken seriously.

Adolescence is a period of serious risk for children of divorce. Again and again, young people reported how much they needed a family structure, how much they longed to be protected, and how much they yearned for clear guidelines for moral behavior.

13-15 years
These years are turbulent at best. The main developmental issues for early teens are these:

❖ They want more freedom than their parents will allow.
❖ They are more likely to listen to their friends' opinions than those of their parents.
❖ They become exceedingly aware of how they look, and they spend a great deal of time trying to look acceptable.
❖ Their opinions often differ from their parents' opinions, and they let their parents know it. If a parent is controlling, this can have violent results.

Teenagers need special support because of their busy and varied schedules. They need their parents to be more flexible and tolerant. For instance, it may be difficult for them to spend an entire weekend with one parent. Parents can give the kids the support they need by being willing to talk about rules, curfews, appropriate friends, allowances, and driving privileges. It's important for teens to know their parents are communicating well with each other when it comes to their welfare and that they cannot play one parent against the other.

16-17 years
These "almost adults" have several developmental tasks to accomplish:

❖ separation from their parents
❖ peer involvement
❖ development of their own identity
❖ sexual identity
❖ development of adult responsibility
❖ career choice and development
❖ independence
❖ moving out

These kids still need parental controls, but they need the controls to be flexible and appropriate for their age. They need to continue meaningful contact with both parents, and they need schedules flexible enough to respect their need to be with friends and involved in their own activities.

It's important that parents be sensitive to their kids' need to be consulted, informed, listened to, and respected without giving up the adult-child relationship.

Angry, weak families are at their most vulnerable during the teenage years. Parents unwittingly make the situation worse by being so preoccupied with their own needs that they don't respond to their teenagers. Also, parents may project their hostile feeling toward an ex-spouse onto their teen—especially mothers onto sons. ("That's disgusting! You're just like your father!")

WEATHERING THE TEEN STORM

Teen years are tough years—for the kids, their parents, and for the entire family. If you have teens in your blended family, expect them to test you with everything they've got.

Allison, a girl of fourteen who looks eighteen, crawled out her bedroom window at 2 a.m. A neighbor who happened to see the girl strolling the streets downtown called her parents.

"Why?" her father demanded when he picked her up.

"I just went for a walk," Allison said. "It was a nice night with a full moon."

"It was stupid!" her father exclaimed. "What's the matter with you, out roaming the streets like that?"

"But there is no one around," Allison said.

"It's dangerous!" her father insisted.

At that Allison bristled. "I can take care of myself, Dad! Why do you treat me like such a baby?"

Kids long for independence, and they are convinced they are totally ready for it. We look at them and we see immaturity and inexperience. They look at us and they see hopeless senility. The final transition to adulthood is tough.

ADULT RELATIONSHIPS

Some problems don't show up until a young person is grown and forming his or her own close relationships with other adults. Take Steve for example. At the age of thirty-two, he continually moves from one sexual involvement to another, never able to make a commitment. "I know this is a dangerous way to live in this day and age," Steve admits. "But the fact is, I have no desire to settle down." His unspoken message is, *My parents couldn't make it in a relationship, so I won't even try.*

Judith Wallerstein's research indicates that a high percentage of young people raised amidst the conflict of divorce break engagements and even leave their would-be spouses standing at the altar. Colleen, sexually active at thirteen, has been engaged three times. Each time, as the wedding date grew near, she broke the engagement.

Some kids model their parents' behavior. Others determine, "no way will I *ever* do that to my family! I will never cause them such pain!" So thoroughly do they rebel against their parents' painful treatment of each other that they go overboard the other way. Nancy recalls a mother she worked with in mediation who immediately gave in to her ex-husband's request for custody. "I don't want to fight it," she told Nancy. "I won't put my children through the horror I was pulled through by my fighting parents."

FUTURE RELATIONSHIPS

In any family, parents are constantly in the process of teaching their children how to parent. Whether they know it or not. Whether they want to or not. Whether they like it or not. For better or for worse, every parent is constantly passing along lessons in parenting.

You say you've made mistakes? Join the crowd. You say you hope and pray your children will grow up to be better parents than you were? So do we.

Let us ask you a question we often use in mediation sessions: *Do you love your children more than you hate your ex-spouse?* If the answer is yes, start today to improve your parenting techniques.

"Well," you may say, "at least I'm a better parent to my kids than my own parents were to me."

Good for you. Are there any of us who have not looked at some of our parents' approaches to parenting and exclaimed, "When I have children, I'll *never* . . ." We see the mistakes our parents made and we vow we'll never subject our little ones to the same errors. And we really mean it. Most people enter parenthood with a

162 CHILDHOOD AND BEYOND

whole list of things they have vowed never to do. Then something happens that triggers the parenting lessons dwelling deep within us, and we find ourselves doing those very same things.

Feeling guilty or constantly berating yourself about not being a good enough parent is not going to do anyone any good. How much better it is to go out and seek resources to help you improve. We can never have too many parenting helps.

Some of the resources you might want to consider are:

- ❖ *Parents Without Partners*
- ❖ *Stepparenting groups*
- ❖ *American Family Organization in Chicago*
- ❖ *American Bar Associations Resource Center for Children* (Washington). They have studies on pilot programs covering various professional practices on a number of issues.
- ❖ *Books on parenting.* See the list of suggested reading in the Appendix. If you can't afford to buy books, look for them in the library.
- ❖ *Speakers and seminars.* Your local junior college is a good resource for speakers on various topics related to parenting. Many also have parent education projects and classes. Various organizations offer seminars and workshops. For example, free seminars are offered by the Marriage Preservation and Divorce Resolution Councils. Their purpose is to help preserve marriages and to help those who have determined to divorce to go through it in an appropriate way.
- ❖ *Mental Health Agencies.* If there is a problem of child abuse or spousal abuse in your family, there are shelters that have counseling available. Also, most areas have mental health agencies that can be a source of help and referrals.

❖ *Caring People*. Ramona, a biracial seven-year-old, doesn't know her father. Her blond-haired, blue-eyed half-sister has a father who picks her up every week and takes her to his house, but not Ramona. Her mother has remarried, and the couple is expecting twin girls in June. Soon Ramona is going to be surrounded by blond sisters with daddies. But Ramona is lucky. A dark-haired uncle has "adopted" her. He takes her to the zoo with his family and buys her ice cream cones and she gets to play with his children. To Ramona, it makes all the difference in the world to have someone just for her.

You are not going to be a perfect parent. Neither are your children. Neither are we. And, yes, we too see the results of our mistakes in our children. Even experts with far more insight than we have occasionally lose it with their kids. They may be stressed out, or they may not be feeling well, or they may have gone over the same instructions to the same kid so many times they can't bear to do it one more time.

Nobody can do everything right. All we can do is the best we can. When you fall down, pick yourself up, apologize, and start moving forward again. When your children become imperfect parents themselves, maybe they'll do the same.

PEACE AT HOME

On her fifteenth birthday, Brigitte told her mother she wanted to live at her father's house.

"Why?" her mom asked. "This has always been your main home. Why do you want to leave us?"

"Because it's crazy here," Brigitte said. "Everybody is mad at everybody, and everyone is always yelling. When I go to Dad's house, I can get some rest."

All of us—you, us, and the experts, too—like to have control within our households. Fortunately, few of our parenting mistakes are fatal. A lot of them can be overcome if we achieve the important parenting goal of peace at home. Make your home a haven of love, security, acceptance, and peace.

Two months after Charlotte and Spencer's divorce was final, Charlotte called Maggie, her stepdaughter. "I want you and your sister and brother to know that you can call me anytime, no matter what, when, where, how, or why," she said. "I will always be your stepmom. I may be divorced from your dad, but my love for you will never change."

"I know that," Maggie said. "I have always known it."

To Charlotte, peace among the family members was a major validation of the investment she had made in the family.

Chapter 11

THE KIDS' VIEW

It Pays to Listen

When Brent is at his dad's house, he has a new jeep to drive to school. But when he is at our house, we have to take him and pick him up. We have no car for him to use, and all the car pools in our neighborhood are filled. It certainly would help us if he were able to bring the jeep over here, but his dad (or stepmom) won't let him.

It's a frustrating situation. When this was Brent's primary residence, we abided by his stepmother's wishes that he be in a car pool in their neighborhood rather than ours so that he could come home to their house and spend time with his little brother. Both ways, we are the ones who do the extra transporting.

"It just seems so complicated trying to deal with this week's transportation," Nancy said to Brent one day.

"Well, you know, Mom, this is just the way it is," Brent answered. "Life has been complicated for me for fourteen years, ever since you and my dad decided to get a divorce."

Brent's right. Things have been complicated for him. They always are for kids in blended families. Even under

the best of circumstances. Even when everyone cooper-
ates and does the best they can.

Throughout this book we have talked about many
aspects of blending families from the viewpoint of the
parents. We thought it might be helpful to look at some
of these issues through the children's eyes.

For children, divorce is a difficult, wrenching experience. Some deny it is happening. Younger children are
frightened, older ones are angry. Some are just very, very
sad. More than a few blame themselves for the family
breakup. Most kids of divorce go through a seesaw of
grief, guilt, abandonment, and sadness.

"WE DON'T BELONG ANYWHERE"

"I live with my mom most of the time," eight-year-old Jarrod said. "Daddy's too busy to take care of me."

"My dad has a new wife and a new baby," Molly said.
"He doesn't need me any more."

Judith Wallerstein found that three out of five children
of divorce felt rejected by at least one of their parents. Like
Molly, they sensed they were a piece of psychological or
economic baggage left over from a regretted journey.

"I love my dad and I love my mom," Lily said. "But I
can't tell my dad I love Mom or he will feel bad, and I
can't tell my mom I love Dad or she will feel bad. I have
to pretend I only *love* the one I'm with and that I only *like*
the other one."

From the child's perspective, keeping parents happy is
always a challenge. Inevitably, at some point and on some
occasion, somebody feels slighted. This concern can lead
to miscommunication and inappropriate assumptions.

Many children stated that moving between two families was a hassle for them.

"That's the part that really bothers me," one teenager
said. "I don't have a place that is strictly my own."

Another added, "Just when I get settled in one place,

I have to get ready to move again. I do a lot of jumping around, and I'm always losing my stuff."

"When I'm not here I miss this family," Brent says. "When I am here I miss the other family."

"My friends never know where to call me," fifteen-year-old Juanita said. "I wish I could afford an answering machine for my telephone so I could just give them one number and then check my messages."

Brent once told Nancy, "You know, Mom, I would be a great roving journalist because I've learned a lot of coping skills going between two homes. It would be nothing to me to go out on the road from place to place."

"I live one week with my dad, the next with my mom, then back to my dad, then back to my mom," said ten-year-old Tyler. "My school is near my dad's house, so when I'm with my mom, I can't play with my friends. It's too far. Mom tells me to just make new friends, but that's not so easy to do. I don't even go to school with the kids here."

In shared parenting, the kids get the great benefit of two parents in their lives. But it can also put a lot of physical and emotional strain on them. It can be even harder on teenagers.

"I don't like having to go to my father's house on weekends," Rachel said. "I want to hang out with my friends. On my weekends there I can't even go to the football games or the Friday night dances. When I complain, my mom says, 'What would you rather do, see your friends that you see all week or see your father?' Well, I'd rather see him some other time and spend the weekends with my friends."

But there are also benefits to living in two families. Brent says, "It's weird, but I get different things out of each family. In this family, we do lots more things together, like going out to movies and stuff. And I spend a lot of time playing with the little kids. At my other house, I have more privacy. I do play with my little brother some, but I mainly do more grown-up things."

"IT'S NOT EVEN OUR FAULT!"

"I always thought we had a good family," Molly said. "Now my dad has a new wife and my mom has a boyfriend and we don't have a family at all."

Most children describe their parents' divorce as the most critical event in their lives. The memories of their parents' breakup remain fresh for a long time.

"I cried when they told me they were getting a divorce," six-year-old Christopher told us. "I begged them to make up and be friends, but they said no. Then they got the divorce."

When adults divorce, they try to shut the door and go on to create a new life. For the child, it is a long process of having to adjust and readjust, first to a failing marriage, then to a separation from parents they still love, then to the animosity that comes with most divorces, then to two post-divorce families. It's a continuing experience with no closed doors and no understandable guidelines.

"Why should we get stuck in the middle?" several children asked. "It's not our fault. We didn't even want the divorce."

"We used to be well-off because my dad had a good job," fifteen-year-old Rachel told us. "He pays some support for my brother and me, but nothing for my mother. The judge told my mom her nice lifestyle was all in the past, that now she could go out and get a job to support herself. But she's never worked, and the only jobs she can get hardly pay anything. We used to live in a nice house and we had a cleaning woman who came in twice a week. Now my mom is a cleaning woman. My brother and I try to help out, but it makes me so mad at my father!"

"HELP US MAKE SENSE OF IT"

When Joanna first came to our house, she would ask, "How come Brent and Nick don't stay here all the time?" The blended family is all Carley has ever known, so it seemed natural to her. But even now, five years later, Joanna still says, "I wonder why Nick goes away so much and I hardly ever get to see him." (This from a child who spent two years in a Bucharest hospital with few visits from family members.)

It's hard for kids to make sense of the changes in their lives. And if parents are willing to listen, some real wisdom can come from the kids. Here are some words of advice children would like to offer their parents:

"Don't tell me bad things about Mommy. I don't want to hear it."

"Try to be nice to each other. You get after us kids when we aren't nice to each other, so why don't you have to be nice?"

"Don't keep buying me toys. It doesn't make me feel any better."

"Why can't you two at least be friends? Why can't we be a family even if you aren't married to each other any more?"

"My mom drives me nuts," Christina told us. "I don't want to hurt her feelings. Why do I have to feel guilty just because I want to see my dad? Mom's got me all year. I only get to see my dad in the summer. Why can't my mom make me feel okay instead of guilty?"

It is confusing. Carley once told Bill she had one brother.

"What do you mean *one brother?*" Bill asked.

"Well," she said, "Brent and Nick aren't my whole brothers, they are my half-brothers. And two halves make a whole!"

Seventeen-year-old Jason had this advice to parents: "Whatever the differences you two have, make sure you take care of them out of range of the kids. Don't let the kids get caught up in your fighting. Try to get along as best you can, although we understand that won't happen all the time. But the thing is, we don't want to be part of your wars."

Juanita adds, "You say you both love us. Okay, then,

act like it. The papers are signed and the divorce is over, so stop the fighting already!"

I FEEL LUCKY

"I have a very good relationship with both my step-mother and my stepfather," Jason told us. "If anything good came out of the divorce, it was that I got two new great parents who have taken care of me and loved me."

"When my mom married Carl, she was the one in charge of rules," said Rebecca, now twenty-one. "I was already sixteen and my brother was fifteen, so we all thought it was best for Carl to stay out of it, and he agreed. Because of Carl and his attitude, my brother and I were blessed with *three* wonderful parents: my mom, my dad, and Carl."

"I was afraid my stepmother wouldn't love me as much as she loved her children," Tyler said. "They are lit-tler and cuter, and they are hers. But she does love me very much. She even lets me get away with stuff sometimes."

Stepbrothers and stepsisters play important roles in the lives of many of the children.

"Nick and I are more like friends than brothers," Brent says. "When we're not together here at the house we go out and do things together. To me, Nick is just a friend who is in the same house as me now and then. Actually, it's pretty convenient!"

One of Brent's reasons for wanting to spend more time at his dad's house was because his little brother Gregory missed him and couldn't understand why Brent was gone so much. We could understand that. Carley and Joanna had a big brother three weeks of the month, and Gregory only had him one week and one weekend.

Gregory idolizes Brent. For years, Brent's carpool to and from school was in their neighborhood, so Brent played with his little brother every afternoon. When I drove up to get Brent, Gregory would run out with him to talk to the girls in the car. He would always ask, "Can I come to your house today?"

The relationship between brothers and sisters, and step-this and step-that, is so different from the relationships between the parents. And many times it holds together in spite of the parents' actions.

"I HATE HIM!"

Not all kids are as enthusiastic about their steprelatives, however. For Natalie, *unenthusiastic* is putting it mildly.

"Dad asked me what I thought about him marrying her, and I told him, 'Lose her, she's a witch,'" Natalie recalled. "But then he went ahead and married her anyway. He asked my opinion, then he did the exact opposite of what I said. I can't understand what he ever saw in her! He should tell her he's going for a walk and never go back."

Many parents make the mistake of giving their children the idea that they have some say in a remarriage. When the child's advice is not followed, the kid feels betrayed. Certainly it is appropriate to get input from an older child, but it should be made perfectly clear that the final decision is the adult's.

Andrea told us, "After my mom died, I did not want Dad to remarry. When he told us he was going to marry Glenda, I decided I would hate her. She would never be *my* mother! I was really scared of having to make more changes. I remember how my sister and I cried, because we were sure Dad would forget Mom."

Andrea's father was wise enough really to listen to his children's fears and concerns. Before the marriage took place, he took his kids to a counselor. While they never welcomed Glenda with open arms, the counselor was able to help all of them prepare for the major adjustment in their family.

We know perfectly well that not all blended family

stories have happy endings. Sad to say, many families never manage to get all the puzzle pieces in place and do not survive as a family. Seventeen-year-old Jackie had this story to tell: "My parents were divorced when I was thirteen, and I was so mad. My dad moved back to Oklahoma and we stayed in Arizona, so I hardly ever saw him. When Mom married Neil, everyone thought he was such a great guy, but I hated him. We got into huge fights, and I called him names and everything. I just hated him! Last year, Mom and Neil got a divorce, so I guess I'd have to say I won."

Jackie graduates from high school this year and is planning to go away to college. Come fall, her mother will be alone. We wonder what Jackie will have to say about her "victory" a few years down the road?

There is much you can do to move your blended family toward success. But one thing you cannot do is demand that one person love another person. People don't love each other because they are ordered to do so. But parents, stepparents, kids, and stepkids all have a right to expect respect from one another. It is a mistake for parents not to lay down that requirement.

"When my mother got married to Jerry, she gave each of us kids a copy of the following contract," Leanna told us:

> "Jerry is not your father, but he is my husband. I expect you to treat him with the same consideration and cooperation as you treat me. I hope you like him, maybe even love him, but you don't have to. You do, however, have to treat him with respect. I think you will find that he has a great deal to offer you.

"Mom let us know this was not just a request, it was a requirement. We did it because we had to. And you know what? Jerry did offer us a great deal. As time went on, we began to truly respect him, and not just because we had to. In time we even learned to love him."

"MAYBE THEY WILL GET BACK TOGETHER"

"I don't want either my mommy or my daddy to get married unless they get married to each other," five-year-old Kelly said. "Maybe they will."

One of the greatest barriers to children accepting their stepparents is that it means giving up the cherished hope that mom and dad will someday get back together. Many children of divorce, even older ones, cling desperately to this fantasy.

"I think my parents might get married again," Jarrod told us. "Dad has a girlfriend, but we hate her. He won't marry her if we hate her."

"I know it isn't very likely that my mom and dad will get back together," Christina said, "but I can always hope, can't I? Stranger things have happened."

Movies such as *Parent Trap* are built upon this theme. Children of divorce nurture the dream that they, like those precocious kids in the movies, will be able to take control and make everything work out so that the old family can all live together again, happily ever after.

You may be saying, "But you tell us to keep our disagreements and conflicts from the kids. Doesn't that just feed their fantasy that things aren't so bad and we might get back together?"

Perhaps. That's why it is important that you address the fantasy and let your children know it is not going to happen. You might say something such as, "Your dad (mom) and I both love you very much. Our love for you is something we always agree on. But we will never again all be a family together. Your dad (mom) and I will never remarry each other."

WHAT ABOUT UNLOVING STEPPARENTS?

"I married Lloyd," Shirley stated, "not his children. His kids are eight, twelve, and fifteen, and I must tell you, I only put up with them because I have to."

We appreciate Shirley's honesty. It is a fact that not all stepparents love their stepchildren, nor are they all committed to doing what is in the children's best interest.

Again, love cannot be mandated. Hopefully the stepparent will be mature enough to treat the child with kindness, patience, and respect. If a child is actually being abused or berated by a stepparent, it is imperative that a professional be called in. The child needs to be protected.

"Shirley would never hurt the kids," Lloyd said. "She just thinks they are a real bother. It's hard for me because I don't know who to support, my wife or the kids."

First and foremost, a parent needs to stay unified with his or her spouse. Parents who take the children's side against the stepparent do great damage to the new family. Lloyd needs to talk seriously with Shirley about the children. It isn't easy to move into a ready-made family. But the children do exist, and they have a right to a relationship with both their father and their mother. That means the stepparent will just have to adjust.

If the children's behavior is making the stepparent's adjustment harder, the children's own parent should talk to them and set down guidelines. For instance, let the children know they can communicate their feelings, but only in an appropriate manner. "I don't like you!" is not appropriate. "I don't like it when you make me go to bed so early" is. Of course, the same guidelines must apply to the parents as well.

For stepparents who are saying, "I'm not a bad person, but I don't love my stepchildren," we have these suggestions:

- ❖ *Go slowly.* Love seldom happens all at once. Start out with "respect" and aim for "like." Let patience be your byword.
- ❖ *Don't set your expectations too high.* Most step-

children don't welcome new stepparents with open arms and hearts. Anticipate difficulties, conflicts, and problems, and do your best to prepare for them.

♣ *Accept differences in personality.* Understand that "different" doesn't mean "worse." Don't demand that your stepchildren be like you—or like your own children. Each child will have his or her own personality, and it may be just the opposite of yours.

♣ *Define your role to your stepchild.* What role do you want to play in the child's life? Companion? Friend? Caregiver? Shopping buddy? Let the child know you are *not* taking the place of a parent. If your relationship thrives and the child begins to view you as a loving parent, wonderful! But let that level of relating evolve slowly and naturally.

♣ *Be clear with your spouse about who will deal with what.* Who disciplines? Who teaches the teenager to drive? Who delegates chores and responsibilities? Who enforces them? Who sets dating rules?

♣ *Don't hold your spouse responsible for your stepchildren's behaviors or personalities.* It's very possible that the things bothering you are also bothering the birth parents. The difference is that they have a higher level of tolerance for their own children.

♣ *Don't give up.* Kids do grow and mature. Often they become more reasonable with age.

Bernice remembers well the years she spent struggling with her stepchildren. "They never actually lived with us, but they were at our house every other weekend and for a month in the summer. I can't tell you how I

176 THE KIDS' VIEW

dreaded those times! The kids didn't like me, and I felt no special love for them. Now they are all grown and married, and the oldest two have children of their own. And an amazing thing has happened. I feel a love for those grandchildren I never felt for the stepchildren." Bernice's love for those grandchildren has strengthened her relationship with her adult stepchildren.

Hang in there. Expect respect and be willing to give it. Give of yourself even when you don't feel like it. You may be surprised at the change of heart that can come with the passing years.

"DO I HAVE TO CHOOSE?"

"When my parents were divorced, I was just eight and my sister was seven," Adam said. "My parents were trying to be fair, but they made us decide how we wanted our schedules between the two families to be. My sister and I talked it over and decided neither Mom nor Dad should have to be alone. So I said my main home would be with my dad and my sister said her main home would be with Mom. When I was one place, my sister was the other place. We hardly saw each other at all, and before long, we hardly knew each other. It was the wrong decision, but we didn't know. We were just little kids. I wish we hadn't had to make the choice."

Many parents think letting the kids choose is the best way to make tough decisions. But please stop to think about it. When faced with a choice of "her or him," what's a child to do?

Lily knows all about that pain. "I hate to choose. I don't want to hurt anyone's feelings, but I always do because when I have to choose, someone is left out."

When you are faced with decisions that affect the kids—custody, weekend visits, summer vacation—by all means ask for their input. Let them share their concern about not being able to get a summer job if they are going to be gone for a month, or of feeling lonely when they are away from their friends, or of worrying about one parent feeling abandoned. Share back and forth, then you parents make the final decision. That's a parent's job.

"TALK AND LISTEN"

"If I could give one piece of advice to kids in blended families, I would say: talk, talk, talk to your parents," Leanna said. "Make sure they know your feelings and your needs. Don't be so afraid of hurting their feelings that you end up hurting yourself. You're in a rough situation, and you have tough decisions to make. You've got to let them know what is best for you."

Jason would agree. "If your parents are doing something that is hurting you, tell them. They probably don't realize it. It's a hard thing to do, but the best way is to be completely open and honest and tell them straight out."

"When I decided I wanted to spend more time at my dad's, I told both my parents that I wanted to make a change in my schedule," Brent said. "It was something I wanted to happen, and they were willing to listen to me."

"My parents were always asking me to do stuff for them while I was at the other house," Natalie said. "My father would say, 'Tell your mother so and so,' or 'Check her calendar when you get home and see if she wrote this or that down.' My mother would say, 'I want you to pick up some things for me while you're in that part of town.' Finally I said, 'Hey, I'm not a messenger here. And it's hard for me to run errands for you. Please don't ask me to do it anymore.' And they didn't."

The kids remind us that the communication has to go both ways.

"Instead of just being mad, they need to tell us what's wrong or what they want from us," Jason said.

Many kids had opinions similar to Molly's: "Parents

should tell kids what's going on. It's our life, too. We need to know!"

"PLEASE BE FLEXIBLE"

Many older kids expressed their frustration at their parents' unwillingness to be flexible with their schedules.

"I'm always having conflicts, like I'm supposed to go to my dad's on Friday but then I'll miss my best friend's party," Natalie said. "I say, 'Can't I go on Saturday morning?' and they say, 'Life's tough. Live with it.'"

"I always miss half the football games because of my visitation schedule," Adam says. "I want to change the schedule through football season, but my parents don't think it's important enough. They say if I was on the team it would be different, but this is just for fun and I should be willing to give up a little fun. It doesn't make me want to visit my dad."

"I'm lucky," Jason said. "My parents understand that I have things of my own, and I need and want to be certain places at certain times. They also tell me when the change makes it really hard on them. I try to be considerate of them, and they are really flexible with me."

"Parents tell us to remember that things are not going to be the same and to try to make the best of it," Jackie said. "They should remember that, too."

WISDOM FROM BRENT

Divorce is hard: I should know. I'm 10 years old and both of my parents are divorced and remarried. Sometimes children think that they caused the divorce by being bad. They think that if they were better behaved that their parents would not divorce. It is wrong to feel that way. People get divorced because they do not get along very well. Just because two parents get divorced, doesn't mean they don't love their child. Parents will always love their child very much.

When my parents were divorced, I was very sad and I

thought it was my fault. Each night after the divorce, I said a short prayer, asking God to help me feel better. Soon I felt a whole lot better. My parents treated me the same as always. Sometimes a child will be mad and pout or even cry. It is all right to feel this way. It will help you feel better.

Children often worry that one of their parents will have to leave and never see them again. That is not right. Parents will always understand and try to work out an even schedule.

—Brent's school journal

It pays to listen to the kids. There's a lot of wisdom in what they say.

Chapter 12

A REAL FAMILY

When the Pieces Come Together

Every Christmas we get a stack of picture Christmas cards from families in which Nancy has placed children for adoption. As babies, all the kids look pretty much alike. But as they grow and develop year after year, we see an amazing thing happen: They often begin to take on the physical characteristics of their adoptive parents, brothers, and sisters. Every year they look more and more like a birth family.

What were once separate families truly can blend together into a unified whole. Each person's personality and character traits remain, but those individualities just make the new family richer and fuller.

"Shortly before my first husband left, he gave me a beautiful amethyst and diamond ring, and a matching amethyst bracelet," Nancy says. "Even though the amethyst is one of my favorite stones, that jewelry lacked luster to me. The timing ruined it. I rarely wore it. When Bill and I had been married a couple of years, our church was having a building drive, and I donated the ring and bracelet to the church.

"The following Christmas, I reached into my Christmas stocking and took out the gifts one at a time, oohing and aahing over each one. When I reached deep into the bottom of the stocking, I was absolutely shocked at what I found. It was the amethyst bracelet and ring. Bill had found out where they were being sold, and he had bought them back. He said, 'Now you can enjoy them because they're from me.'"

Blended families have the unique opportunity to take the pieces of their lives that seem dull and ruined, and to watch them be rejuvenated into beautiful, lustrous jewels. Your children are diamonds. Your stepchildren are amethysts. And your new spouse is the one who brings them all together with you.

"When I remarried seven years ago, my children were teenagers," Rosemary said. "My husband had three children ranging in age from twelve to sixteen. The kids were always arguing and bickering over who was a *real* parent and who wasn't real.

"My husband tried hard to be a good stepfather to my kids, and I did my best with his kids when they were with us. But they all loved to say, 'You aren't my *real* parent, and I don't have to do what you say.'"

Rosemary and her husband each sat down with their own children and told them: "I love you so much, but you must understand I also love my spouse. We are not playing a game of who loves who more here. In a family, everybody loves everybody, and everyone treats everyone else with caring and respect. It's important for you to understand that my love for you does not affect my right to be married to someone I love and who loves me."

Rosemary and her husband's blended family have weathered some rocky times, but they have emerged a *real* family.

"If we could only realize that we are all *real*, that no one in a blended family is invisible, then we would be able to heal," Rosemary said. Then she added: "Every one of us is given an opportunity to learn so much from each other. Why should we limit the number of people we allow into our lives?"

Why indeed?

Here is the message from our blended family to yours: Whether your child was born to you or not, be a real parent. When you work toward blending your family, be persistent but patient, firm but flexible, level-headed but loving.

We know there are going to be times of frustration and discouragement in your family. There are in ours. That's why Nancy keeps her "Joy Box" handy. When we get encouraging notes, when we get words of love and appreciation from the children, we put them into the box. When we need to be uplifted, we pull them out one by one and soak up the encouragement:

"I will never, ever try to hurt you, Mom. I will love you forever!"

"Thank you for being the best mom and dad in the world."

"My family, by Joanna," carefully printed in red crayon over her hand-drawn picture of our family—all seven of us, including Brent and Nick.

Snippets from Nick's project from his cinematography class entitled, "My Life." Although he lives mainly with his mom, he proudly shows all of us off as his family.

Valentines signed with XOXOXO. Handmade cards carefully colored with crayon. Childish expressions of love and appreciation. Tear-stained notes that plead, "I'm so sorry. Please forgive me," and notes that joyfully proclaim, "Thank you, thank you, thank you. I love you!"

The pieces of your family puzzle can be put back together in such a way that a beautiful picture will emerge. Embrace the evidence of your successes and progress, and move forward together. You *are* a real family. Congratulations on how far you have come!

Appendix

SUGGESTED READING

Berman, Clare. *Making it as a Stepparent: New Roles/New Rules.* New York: Doubleday, 1980.

Erickson, Marilyn S. McKnight. *The Children's Books: For the Sake of the Children.* West Concord: CPI Publishing, 1992.

Galper, M.A. *Joint Custody and Co-Parenting: Sharing Your Child Equally.* Philadelphia: Running Press, 1980.

Morgenbesser, M., and N. Nehls. *Joint Custody.* Chicago: Nelson-Hall, 1981.

Paris, Erna. *Stepfamilies: Making Them Work.* New York: Avon, 1984.

Ricci, Isodora. *Mom's House, Dad's House: Making Shared Custody Work.* New York: MacMillian, 1980.

Wallerstein, Judith S., Ph.D., and Sandra Blakeslee, *Second Chances: Men, Women & Children a Decade After Divorce.* New York: Ticknor and Fields, 1989.

Ware, Ciji. *Shared Parenthood After Divorce: An Enlightened Study Guide for Mothers, Fathers and Children.* New York: Bantam Books, 1984.

AUTHORS

NANCY S. PALMER, a board certified marital and family lawyer and past chair of the family lawyers in Florida, left a successful law practice to mediate and help others parent after divorce. She trains mediators around the country and currently serves as co-chair of the Alternative Dispute Resolution Committee of the Family Law Section of the American Bar Association. Nancy is the coauthor of *When Your Ex Won't Pay: Getting Your Kids the Financial Support They Deserve* (Piñon Press, 1995).

WILLIAM D. PALMER is a certified civil and family mediator who practices in the areas of litigation, family law, and appeals. He has been an attorney with the Orlando office of Carlton, Fields, Ward, Emmanuel, Smith & Cutler, P.A. since 1976. Bill and Nancy parent a blended family of five children: Brent, Nicholas, Michelle, Carley, and Joanna.

KAY MARSHALL STROM has written thirteen books and contributed to many others. She is president of Santa Barbara Literary Service, an editing and critiquing service for writers. When she isn't writing, Kay teaches writing classes and speaks at seminars and special events throughout the country. She and her husband, Larry, are the parents of two young adults.